Poets of the Apocalypse

Twayne's English Authors Series

Kinley E. Roby, Editor

Northeastern University

TEAS 360

BATTLE OF BRITAIN
Painting by Paul Nash.
*Reproduced by permission of
The Trustees of the Imperial
War Museum, London.*

Poets of the Apocalypse

By Arthur Edward Salmon
University of Idaho

Twayne Publishers • Boston

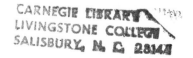

Poets of the Apocalypse

Arthur Edward Salmon

Copyright © 1983 by G. K. Hall & Company
All Rights Reserved
Published by Twayne Publishers
A Division of G. K. Hall & Company
70 Lincoln Street
Boston, Massachusetts 02111

Book Production by John Amburg
Book Design by Barbara Anderson

Printed on permanent/durable acid-free
paper and bound in the United States of
America.

Library of Congress Cataloging in Publication Data

Salmon, Arthur Edward.
    Poets of the apocalypse.

    (Twayne's English authors series ; TEAS 360)
    Bibliography: p. 140
    Includes index.
    1. English poetry—20th century—History and criticism.
2. Apocalyptic literature—History and criticism.
3. Anarchism and anarchists in literature.
4. Hendry, J. F.—Criticism and interpretation.
5. Treece, Henry, 1911–1966—Criticism and interpretation.
I. Title. II. Series.
PR610.S34   1983   821'.912'093   82-23218
ISBN 0-8057-6846-7

Contents

About the Author
Preface
Acknowledgments
Chronology

Chapter One
Introduction: The Inward Gaze   1

Chapter Two
James F. Hendry: Apocalyptic Poet and Apologist   23

Chapter Three
Henry Treece   43

Chapter Four
Apocalyptic Associates: MacCaig, Fraser, and Moore   62

Chapter Five
Personalism   85

Chapter Six
Libertarian and Neo-Romantic Parallels   91

Chapter Seven
Conclusion   116

Notes and References   129
Selected Bibliography   140
Index   145

About the Author

Arthur Edward Salmon received the doctorate from the University of Wisconsin at Madison, where he majored in English Literature and minored in Theater and Drama. His Master of Arts degree in English Literature is from the University of Illinois at Champaign-Urbana. He now teaches courses in contemporary literature and the literature of Western civilization at the University of Idaho at Moscow.

Before coming to the University of Idaho, Professor Salmon taught at the University of Wisconsin's Madison campus, Center-System campus at Wausau, Wisconsin, and the University of Dubuque. At the University of Dubuque, he taught a broad spectrum of courses, including interdisciplinary courses which he created and which carried credit in four different departments and covered five areas: English, Political Science, Psychology, and Philosophy and Religious Studies. He also taught more traditional courses in modern drama and modern British literature. At the University of Wisconsin's Madison campus, for three years he taught courses in modern British and American literature and composition. At the University of Wisconsin's Center-System campus at Wausau, he taught courses in modern British and American literature.

Preface

"Of all the anthologies of the war period," writes Derek Stanford, " . . . none can have proved so influential as *The White Horseman,* with its plum-coloured cloth covers and green spine." It was the second anthology of the British Apocalyptic Movement, which was headed by J. F. Hendry and Henry Treece. *Poets of the Apocalypse* is about Hendry and Treece and several related poets associated with the Apocalyptic Movement, Personalism—a literary movement which developed partly out of the Apocalyptic Movement under the direction of Treece and Stefan Schimanski—and Neo-Romanticism, which eventually incorporated both the Apocalyptic Movement and Personalism.

The implications of the concept of *apocalypse* have been largely ignored or misunderstood by literary critics such as Frederick Hoffman, George Orwell, Stephen Spender, and Francis Scarfe. In Freudian language, the term *apocalypse,* like Romanticism, is "overdetermined" or has multiple associations. For Hendry, *apocalypse* primarily means a philosophy of social collapse, as Chapter 2 indicates.

In addition, the word *apocalypse,* perhaps not coincidentally, strictly means *revelation,* as D. H. Lawrence reminds us in his *Apocalypse.* It is a meaning which agrees with the function of Apocalyptic art, as announced by Treece and G. S. Fraser, as a revelation of unconscious processes.

But the actual *art* of poets such as Treece and Hendry sometimes represents a revival of an older tradition of apocalyptic writing going back to Shelley, Blake, and Langland. Vernon Watkins may be considered an Apocalyptic poet because some of his poems are included in the Apocalyptic anthologies, or because, as T. E. Helmstadter notes, Watkins also attaches importance to "myth as a means towards understanding human needs." But Watkins, who serves as an example here, is also an apocalyptic (with a small *a*) poet in a more historical sense. He shares in the popular fascination with the concept of apocalypse evident in the cinema since *The Four Horsemen of the Apocalypse* (1921) and in evangelical Christianity, which gains its enthusiasm about the concept of apocalypse largely from Christ's eschatological sayings and other Old and New Testament references to end times. Moreover, apocalyptic visions in poetry in the 1940s incorporate doomsday imagery often to suggest symbolically not the end of the world, but the end of one sort of world and the beginning of another. The renewed world was sometimes Marxist, but often anarchist in character.

Although anecdotal books on the 1940s have appeared, little has been written to explain the Neo-Romantic art of the 1940s, or to provide an overview or overviews of it; and the anarchist tradition in art and philosophy which Apocalypticism, Personalism, and the larger Neo-Romanticism reflect has not been treated by literary critics. Sir Herbert Read's influence on Apocalypticism was clearly acknowledged at the outset by Henry Treece, however, and is therefore briefly noted by later writers. A more thoroughgoing treatment of Read's influence on the poetry of the 1940s is needed, but one which also recognizes the anarchist tradition behind the literature of the 1940s generally. Hendry, Treece, Read, Wrey Gardiner, Alex Comfort, Derek Stanford, and other Neo-Romantics, as well as related anarchists, like George Woodcock, consciously or unconsciously extend into the poetry of the 1940s an anarchist perspective that goes back to Tolstoy, Thoreau, Peter Kropotkin, William Godwin, and the anarchist-apocalyptic poems of Shelley, such as *Hellas* and *Prometheus Unbound*.

Chapter 1 is introductory, and for the historical parts of it I have relied on the recollections of some of the poets involved in the events described. Read's Neo-Romantic status and influence upon the literary movements of the 1940s is also treated in Chapter 1, and to a lesser extent throughout the text.

The art of Neo-Romantics such as Hendry and Comfort is varied and diverse, and many of the writers discussed in the following pages warrant book-length treatment. My approach has been limited to their apocalyptic characteristics and association with Apocalypticism in particular and Neo-Romanticism in general in essentially the 1940s.

Arthur Edward Salmon

University of Idaho

Acknowledgments

Grateful acknowledgment is made to J. F. Hendry for permission to quote from the Apocalyptic anthologies and his works, to Nicholas Moore, George Woodcock, and Wrey Gardiner for permission to quote from their works, and to Paddy Fraser to quote from the works of G. S. Fraser. Grateful acknowledgment is made also for permission to quote from the following sources. Henry Treece's *Invitation and Warning* (1942) and *The Black Seasons* (1945): reprinted by permission of Faber and Faber Ltd. Herbert Read's *Collected Poems,* copyright 1966: reprinted by permission of the publisher, Horizon Press, New York. Dylan Thomas's *Poems of Dylan Thomas;* copyright 1938, 1939 by New Directions Publishing Corporation; copyright 1945 by the Trustees for the Copyrights of Dylan Thomas; copyright 1952 by Dylan Thomas: reprinted by permission of New Directions Publishing Corporation. Kingsley Amis's *A Case of Samples* (1957): reprinted by permission of Curtis Brown, Ltd., copyright © 1956 by Kingsley Amis. Norman MacCaig's *Far Cry* (London, 1943) and *The Inward Eye* (London, 1946): reprinted by permission of Routledge and Kegan Paul Ltd. "No Escape" and "Birds All Singing" from Norman MacCaig's *Riding Lights* (1955): reprinted by permission from the author and Chatto & Windus Ltd. "Church Going," "Lines on a Young Lady's Photograph Album," "Triple Time," "Toads," and "Poetry of Departures": reprinted from Philip Larkin's *The Less Deceived* (1955) by permission of The Marvell Press, England. For copies of letters to Henry Treece, I am gratefully indebted to Mrs. Francis Helmstadter, who has provided the copies from the files of her late husband, Professor Thomas Helmstadter. For historical material at the beginning of Chapter 1, especially, and throughout the book, I am also indebted to information graciously provided by J. F. Hendry, Wrey Gardiner, George Woodcock, J. Meary Tambimuttu, Nicholas Moore, John Bayliss, Roland Gant, and Alex Comfort.

Chronology

1924   *Speculations: Essays on Humanism and the Philosophy of Art by T. E. Hulme,* edited by Sir Herbert Read.

1926   Read's *Reason and Romanticism.*

1931   Read's *Wordsworth;* D. H. Lawrence's *Apocalypse.*

1933   Read's *Art Now,* which helped to establish Read as the major British authority on modern art.

1934   Dylan Thomas's *18 Poems.* Read's *Art and Industry.*

1935   Sir Herbert Read's *Poems, 1914–1934* by Faber and Faber and *The Green Child,* a Neo-Romantic novel; David Gascoyne's *A Short Survey of Surrealism.*

1936   In London the Surrealist exhibition is attended by Dylan Thomas, Read, J. F. Hendry, and Breton, and Read's *Surrealism,* an anthology accompanying the exhibition, is published by Faber and Faber. Thomas's *25 Poems.*

1938   Henry Treece meets Thomas; Nicholas Moore begins publishing *Seven,* from which "indirectly—The New Apocalypse was born." Moore, John Goodland, Dorian Cooke, and later, Treece and J. F. Hendry, plan an anthology of Apocalyptic literature. Hendry in his apartment in Leeds works on a manifesto. Thomas agrees to be included in the first Apocalyptic anthology, but refuses to sign the manifesto.

1939   Hendry determines the content of the first Apocalyptic anthology; for the poetry section, Hendry includes Thomas, Norman MacCaig, Cooke, Treece, and Moore; Hendry finds a publisher, Fortune Press, for *The New Apocalypse,* edited by Hendry and Treece and the first Apocalyptic anthology. On 23 August Russia signs a ten-year nonaggression pact with Germany, weakening the credibility of Marxist writers of the 1930s. On 1 September Germany invades Poland and annexes Danzig.

1940 Hendry sees Herbert Read about Routledge & Kegan Paul's publishing *The White Horseman*. In Billiericay, Essex, Wrey Gardiner founds the Grey Walls Press, which published most of the Neo-Romantics. Gardiner meets Alex Comfort. Treece's *38 Poems*. Read's *Annal of Innocence* and *Experience*. Dunkirk evacuation, 26 May to 3 June. Battle of Britain begins 10 July.

1941 George Woodcock begins publishing his *Now*, a literary magazine including writers such as Kathleen Raine, George Barker, Paul Goodman, Alex Comfort, D. S. Savage, and Herbert Read. Barker's *Selected Poems* and Spender's *Ruins and Visions*. Treece becomes poetry editor of *Kingdom Come*. *The White Horseman*, the Movement's second anthology, is published by Routledge & Kegan Paul, where Sir Herbert Read is a director. It includes the poetry of Treece, Hendry, Tom Scott, Vernon Watkins, and MacCaig.

1942 *Lyra: An Anthology of New Lyric,* edited by Robert Greacen and Alex Comfort. *Lyra* includes John Bayliss, G. S. Fraser, Wrey Gardiner, Robert Greacen, Robert Herring, Nicholas Moore, J. Meary Tambimuttu, Treece, Vernon Watkins, and Peter Wells. Hendry's *The Bombed Happiness,* a collection of his poems. Treece's *Invitation and Warning,* a collection of poems.

1943 Comfort and John Bayliss begin publication of *New Road: New Directions in European Art and Letters,* which includes G. S. Fraser, Wrey Gardiner, David Gascoyne, Sidney Keyes, Nicholas Moore, D. S. Savage, Tambimuttu, Treece, Watkins, Stefan Schimanski, George Woodcock, André Breton, and others. *Transformation,* edited by Treece and Stefan Schimanski, the first Personalist anthology. It includes Read, Hendry, Treece, and Fraser. Wrey Gardiner's *The Once Loved God.* Hendry's *The Orchestral Mountain: A Symphonic Elegy. Scottish Short Stories,* edited by Hendry and his wife, Theodora. In September, the Allies sign an armistice with Italy.

1944 *Transformation Two,* edited by Treece and Schimanski. *New Road: New Directions in European Art and Letters,* edited by

Comfort and John Bayliss, and *The Crown and the Sickle,* edited by Treece and Hendry, which includes short stories by Comfort and Fred Marnau, and poetry by Comfort, Treece, Hendry, Peter Wells, Cooke, Gardiner, Robert Greacen, and others. *Herbert Read: An Introduction to His Work by Many Hands,* edited by Henry Treece.

1945   Treece's *The Black Seasons. Transformation Three,* edited by Treece and Schimanski. Hendry's *The Blackbird of Ospo: Stories of Jugoslavia.* On 29 April, the 7th Army reaches Dachau concentration camp. In May, Germany surrenders.

1946   Comfort's *Art and Social Responsibility,* probably the most theoretically developed manifesto of the Neo-Romantic Movement. *Transformation Four,* edited by Treece and Schimanski, the last Personalist anthology. Treece's *How I See Apocalypse.*

1949   *A New Romantic Anthology,* edited by Treece and Schimanski and published by Wrey Gardiner's Grey Walls Press. The last major Neo-Romantic anthology, it includes Read, Moore, Spender, Watkins, Comfort, Hendry, G. S. Fraser, Keidrych Rhys, Thomas, Watkins, etc.; Comfort's "An Exposition of Irresponsibility," from which *Art and Social Responsibility* develops; and Read's "On Romanticism." Hendry's *Fernie Brae: A Scottish Childhood,* a partly autobiographical novel. Treece's *Dylan Thomas: "Dog Among the Fairies,"* the first book of literary criticism on Thomas.

1956   *New Lines,* edited by Robert Conquest and Kingsley Amis, an anthology of poets of "The Movement," a reaction against the New Apocalypse and the wider Neo-Romanticism of the 1940s.

Chapter One

Introduction:
The Inward Gaze

The Literary Scene

"The New Apocalypse was a well organized movement of the continental type," Kenneth Rexroth writes in his Introduction to *The New British Poets* (1949). But the Apocalyptic Movement was less well organized than Rexroth imagined. The idea for it grew out of the work of Nicholas Moore (a son of the philosopher G. E. Moore), John Goodland, and Dorian Cooke on the magazine *Seven,* which published the early works of other writers associated with the New Apocalypse: J. F. Hendry, Henry Treece, Norman MacCaig, and G. S. Fraser. "Fraser I met at St. Andrews, and . . . when I started my magazine *Seven* in 1938, he was immediately a contributor," Moore recalls, adding, "Treece I never met, but I accepted a rather large batch of his poems for *Seven,* and from that—indirectly—The New Apocalypse was born."[1]

John Goodland, who started out as a coeditor of *Seven* with Moore, later designated himself merely as publisher. He had attended a Quaker school with Moore and later Cambridge, where the two planned *Seven.* Goodland was "not exactly 'a rich Quaker,' " as reported in earlier criticism. Religion was "the first Weltanschauung to dissatisfy him," Moore notes. *Seven* also failed to retain his interest, perhaps because he became "inflamed with passion for a sophisticated lady journalist from Düsseldorf (she swore that she wasn't a Nazi and that Düsseldorf intellectuals were a hotbed of anti-Nazi resistance) who later transferred her Mata Hari–Marlene Dietrich like affections" to another of Moore's old-school friends.[2]

Goodland's interest in finding an acceptable Weltanschauung also helped to separate him from Moore and *Seven,* but drew him toward Dorian Cooke and J. F. Hendry. Cooke was a "down-and-out ex-student from Leeds University." Goodland took Cooke "under his wing," allowing him to sleep "on the floor of a ramshackled bed with his girl-friend Wendy on the completely bare boards of the loft" Goodland rented in Inglebert Street in London for the distribution of *Seven*.[3] Cooke was designated by Goodland as the distributor. Later, Cooke's poetry and fiction would appear in *The New Apocalypse*.

Moore believes that it was from Cooke's "fertile imagination that the idea of a group" developed. It was an idea "calculated to appeal to Goodland's Weltanschauung interests." Cooke went to see Treece about the formation of such a group and came back to report to Moore and Goodland. "I think I am correct more or less about the origins of the movement," Moore notes. "From the point when Dorian Cooke went to see Treece the idea was in the air, and from then on Treece and Hendry took over." Moore "went along with the idea partially and somewhat half-heartedly," partly because of his lack of interest in the kind of literary movement which might tend to impose "a conformity of manner and a fashion of rightness." Consequently, he became the "doubter in the party, particularly when the name for it, The New Apocalypse, cropped up." He was interested in promulgating "only what was well-written, not the ideas behind it."[4] "My ideas of what was required were nothing like what it became in the hands of Hendry and Treece and, later, Schimanski," Moore recollects. "Hendry and Treece were its leaders, though not its founders. As far as I was concerned they took over the idea of a projected movement that was under discussion and led it astray!"[5] Hendry and Treece were able to take over because the "literary aspect of it was somewhat over the head of Goodland" and Cooke "was young, broke and unknown."[6]

Hendry himself acknowledges that the *Seven* group developed the concept of a movement, but "only vaguely": "I pirated nothing." Moore, Cooke, and Goodland "had the magazine, but were not sure where they were going and were regarded as amateurs."[7] He met Cooke independently and accidentally. In 1938 Hendry was living in Leeds with his wife and child. Dorian, he recalls, appeared on his doorstep one evening, asking, " 'Is Dylan Thomas living here?' " He was not, but Cooke was to become one of Hendry's frequent visitors. Hendry "put him up" for a while until Cooke got an apartment for himself "around the corner." It was out of discussions held in Hendry's Leeds apartment that the Apocalyptic Movement developed in its final form. Henry Treece, who was to edit all three Apocalyptic anthologies with Hendry and to become the movement's most important poet, and Keidrych Rhys, who passed himself off as Dylan Thomas to get drinks at the local pubs, also became frequent visitors. These writers discussed with Hendry "the contemporary literary scene" and, Hendry observes, "were unhappy about the way things were moving in politics and law" and about the apparent polarization of the world into "two sides."[8]

The "machine age," they felt, "was responsible for almost everything," Hendry comments in a recent interview. "There is a very interesting analysis of the German attack on France in 1914 by one of our historians," Hendry notes, "in which he says that the Kaiser wanted to stop the war. But the trains had moved to the front with the ammunition and the men, and you couldn't stop them." Technology and the machine state had, again, gotten out of control. "So as I say, we didn't consider ourselves as machine smashers," but "wanted people to understand that this [the machine] is only a tool and it's got to be controlled." Such antimechanistic conclusions Hendry continues to advocate. The more recent effect of Russian or American "technology" in the developing countries has been to "smash the local culture altogether, New Guinea, and everywhere. And to smash it—for heaven's sake—in the name of civilization."[9]

Such antimechanistic sentiments also became a central part of the Apocalyptic manifesto conceptualized in Hendry's apartment in Leeds on 11 December 1938. Refuting earlier confusion about who attended this important meeting, Hendry observes that "Nicholas Moore wasn't there at all. . . . MacCaig wasn't there at all." Rather, "Treece and I and Goodland were the ones who, with Dorian Cooke, tried to hammer out this manifesto, so to speak."[10] The so-called manifesto is quoted by subsequent critics, such as Francis Scarfe in *Auden and After,* and by Treece and Stefan Schimanski in *A New Romantic Anthology.* In it Hendry includes the following points:

(1) That Man was in need of greater freedom, economic no less than aesthetic, from machines and mechanistic thinking.
(2) That no existent political system, Left or Right . . . was able to provide this freedom.

(3) That the Machine Age had exerted too strong an influence on art, and had prevented the individual development of Man.
(4) That Myth, as a personal means of reintegrating the personality, had been neglected and despised.

Cooke's enthusiasm for Dylan Thomas helped to insure Thomas's influence on the Apocalyptic Movement. In fact, Cooke's idea for a literary movement had been in part calculated to appeal to Goodland and Treece's interest in Thomas.[11] Treece and Goodland attempted to persuade Thomas to join the movement, in effect, by signing the "manifesto." Although George Orwell would later describe Thomas as an Apocalyptic poet, as would G. S. Fraser and Alex Comfort, Thomas in a letter dated 31 December 1938 to Treece notes that he "won't sign." More cautious than Moore and Fraser in the late 1930s about becoming associated (and therefore labeled) with any literary movement, Thomas writes to Treece: "I wouldn't sign any manifesto unless I had written every word of it, and then I might be too ashamed."
Earlier in 1939, upon seeing Goodland in London, Thomas had apparently told him that the "manifesto" was " 'complete balls.' "[12] Hendry was infuriated. When asked whether he had ever talked to Thomas about this remark, Hendry responded that he had, "once, in a pub in Soho, when he [Thomas] backed down."[13] Thomas's language in his 31 December 1938 letter to Treece is similarly metaphoric. Apparently alluding to language in the unpublished first draft of the manifesto about organic approaches to art and politics, Thomas informs Treece, ". . . that the language of such documents is strange to me, that organic reality is all my cock." But he adds that he would be "very glad to write for Apocalypse. . . ." Two of Thomas's works, a poem and a short story entitled "The Burning Baby," are, as a consequence, included in *The New Apocalypse*.
The problem the Apocalyptic group faced was finding a publisher. Faber and Faber was the "classiest publisher" of verse, and every young poet "wanted if possible to be published by Faber."[14] Fortune Press was an alternative. It was run by Caton, who impressed many of the poets of the period as a kind of Dickensian scoundrel. He was "a rather unsavoury little man who ran gay pornography as a side-

show," Alex Comfort recalls, adding, "I once had to threaten to beat him up in his office to get a MS back. . . ."[15]

Hendry and Treece's reactions were similar. Mr. Caton was a "very unsavoury character whom I was trying to sue before going to Yugoslavia in late 1939," Hendry recalls.[16] In a 15 September 1941 letter to Comfort, Treece maintains that Caton "is unbalanced" and "lives in a world of mistrust, and is fond of inventing lies." Treece adds, "He has also spread the rumour that I am 'queer,' alternating with the sop that I am a nice fellow and Hendry is the wolf." In a more jocular 18 October 1941 letter to Comfort, he exclaims, "Hooray that Caton has lost his typewriter! He can't lose his honour or his pride—he never had them."[17]

The New Apocalypse was published by Caton at Fortune Press. Understandably, Treece and Hendry wanted to find a different publisher for the second Apocalyptic anthology, *The White Horseman*. Hendry wanted Faber. But he was successful at Routledge & Kegan Paul, where Sir Herbert Read was a director: "I was the one who went to London to interview Read about the book" Hendry notes, "and I think that he felt the Movement was going to be quite important. As a matter of fact, he was always very sympathetic." Read suggested including Vernon Watkins,[18] probably because his Neo-Romantic credentials seemed already well established. Read would have seen the developing Apocalyptic Movement as another manifestation of the nineteenth-century Romantic tradition, which is largely what it was.

Before the third Apocalyptic anthology was published in 1944, it was evident to a number of perceptive observers that a new Romanticism was developing, apparently related to Dylan Thomas's work, and that Apocalypticism was a part of it. Wrey Gardiner remembers having by autumn 1942 reviewed one of Treece's anthologies in which Treece "saw some evidence of a new romanticism," most of the Neo-Romantic poets being "unknown to each other and so not constituting a clique but a fairly broad section of the younger writers of that time." Gardiner wrote in his editorial that " 'no better words could be found to describe the poems we print in *Poetry Quarterly*.' " He also noted that this "interesting development" was being watched in the United States, as indicated by a letter he had received from Oscar Williams.[19] *Poetry: A Magazine of Verse* would later devote es-

sentially an entire issue (March 1947) to Neo-Romantic poets:[20]
Treece, Vernon Watkins, and Hendry, as well as Thomas and Barker,
who could now be explicitly identified as Neo-Romantics as well as
Neo-Romantic forerunners.

The leading publisher of the Neo-Romantics was Grey Walls
Press, which belonged to Wrey Gardiner.[21] He was "a natural hippie
before his time," who "had wandered all over as a single-handed
yachtsman and had an endless succession of nice motherly ladies who
found him in need of protection."[22] Gardiner ran a bookshop in Billiericay, Essex, twenty-five miles from London, where he founded his
Grey Walls Press in 1940. One of his friends and associates was Alex
Comfort. It was "a very strange co-incidence," Gardiner recalls, that
Dr. Alex Comfort was in 1940 at a local hospital in Billiericay, where
Comfort had gone to join the evaucated London Hospital. Another
"co-incidence" was that Denise Levertov, the poet, was working at
the same hospital as a nurse. "They were both naturally attracted to
my office in the Elizabethan house known as Grey Walls. Hence the
name of the Press."[22] In 1946, Grey Walls Press combined with Falcon Press, run by Peter Baker, who became a conservative member of
Parliament, recalls Roland Gant, who joined the group after the
merger. Baker, whose father was a managing director of Ealing films,
thought he could publicize books as one publicizes films, and, making other business blunders, Gant notes, eventually brought about
the financial collapse of both Falcon Press and Grey Walls Press.[23]

Gardiner's main interest was the magazine *Poetry Quarterly,* and
Comfort was instrumental in helping him improve the quality of *Po-
etry Quarterly* by giving him the manuscripts of young poets from
Cambridge University who had been his friends.[24] One of them was
Nicholas Moore, who in the 1940s also worked for Grey Walls Press
in London with Comfort and Gardiner. Comfort's own *Lyra: An Anthology of New Lyric,* which he coedited with Robert Greacen, *New
Road: New Directions in European Art and Letters,* which he coedited
with John Bayliss, and *Poetry Folios,* which he coedited with Peter
Wells—at Langham, Wells and Comfort printed the first *Poetry Folio*
on a hand press—combined anarchopacifists, such as George Woodcock, Surrealists, and Apocalyptics.

Moore worked also for J. Meary Tambimuttu's *Poetry* (London).
"Tambi was my friend," Moore observes, and he "quickly got in

touch with me" to work on *Poetry*. The "seer of Marchmont Street and later of Manchester Square," Tambi was part of the literary social life of London. Moore, who "occasionally went round with him and his friends," recalls that Tambi "used to roam from pub to pub with an incredible collection of hopefuls, scroungers, hangers-on and prospective backers, and a few friends too." Like Dylan Thomas, "Tambi himself, of course, was also a sought celebrity," and "people going round on the scene would want to get close to Dylan or get close to Tambi, much as later younger pop fans would want to get close to Elvis or Bob Dylan (Zimmerman—he took his name from Dylan)." A Tamil prince from Ceylon, Tambi's "mystical Eastern gobbledegook (or nearly all of it)" was "for public consumption," Moore observes. He "suffered in much the same way as Dylan. He had to be the centre of the scene, because he had to get backers for his projects (and in each case there was also a boll-weevilish 'looking for a home' element)."[25]

George Woodcock's anarchist *Now*, started on Easter Sunday 1940, also published Comfort (who was on *Now's* editorial board for one issue), Kathleen Raine, Paul Goodman, George Barker, Kenneth Rexroth, Peter Wells, Roy Fuller, D. S. Savage, Julian Symons, Herbert Read, and others with antiestablishment perspectives. Woodcock in turn wrote for *Poetry Quarterly, New Road, Kingdom Come* ("more Surrealist than Apocalyptic," Comfort believes), and *Poetry Folios*, as well as publishing with Grey Walls Press.

Woodcock often "ate and drank" with Gardiner "on the Soho Circuit" and knew Dylan Thomas "quite well," although "as a drinking companion rather than a close friend." But he knew Thomas enough "to vouch that he wrote his poetry in cold sobriety." "There was indeed a period," Woodcock adds, when Thomas "began to work for the BBC, when Dylan took on an awful bureacratic pomposity, wearing a Homburg hat, carrying a briefcase and greeting his drinking companions with great condescension, but this was fortunately very temporary." But a "great deal of friendly intercourse went on among poets of all kinds in Soho and Fitzrocia," Woodcock recalls, "where we mingled in the Bohemian pubs and cafés: the Helvetia, the French House (York Minster), the Café Royal, Fama's Bertorelli's, the Café Bleu, etc., etc."[26] Gardiner remembers Comfort and Moore often having coffee together near Gardiner's office in Bloomsbury to discuss

literary matters. Around and in the background were a "wild under-
growth of would-be-poets, would-be-editors with their magazines."[27]

The "climate" of the war "was odd," notes Comfort, who recalls
that some poets "were in the Forces and, at that time, kicking their
heels on guard duty, only the Navy and the RAF being in actual
combat." Some poets were conscientious objectors "doing farm work
at communes like Langham (run by John Middleton Murry, a most
unpleasant pseud., who made his living by peddling his wife Katherine Mansfield's bones from a handcart, metaphorically, of course, as
I once told him to his face)." "Others were weirder—Tambimuttu
from Ceylon, a visitor to whose pad found a pound of (scaree!) butter
in the bed, Wrey Gardiner's formidable, blind old mother standing
over the workman who was cutting down her railings to make tanks
with a bucket of water and a fire extinguisher. . . ."[28] Julian Symons,
D. S. Savage, and George Woodcock, as the pages of *Now* make
clear, were conscientious objectors. For a while Woodcock worked as
a conscientious objector "on the land in Cambridgeshire" with Nicholas Moore.[29]

Henry Treece joined the Royal Air Force, but did not see action.
Dorian Cooke became "excitingly associated with Tito's Yugoslav
partisans in the war."[30] On 3 September, Britain and France declared
war on Germany. Hendry, who on 4 September 1939 vaguely writes
to Treece that his "spring has dried up like my throat," had secretly
been given an "intelligence job in the Balkans." "I landed in France
before the troops boarded the Orient Express," he observes.

He returned from Yugoslavia in January 1940, and by May 1940
he was in London,[31] which was "intact" but "disfigured by huts and
pill-boxes" and "sandbagged." The Battle of Britain, which began on
10 July 1940, was "confined to the South—there was bomb damage,
mostly around airfields, and civilians saw combat chiefly as skeins of
vapour trails."[32] On 12 August 1940, Portsmouth was bombed. The
London Blitz began with an all-night raid on London on 20 August,
and on 25 August the RAF made its first raid on Berlin. "Denise
Levertov and I used to sit in pubs in London during the blitz talking
about poetry," Gardiner recalls.[33] Hendry and his wife, Theodora,
also witnessed the fire-bombing of London.

On 10 December 1941, Treece wrote to Comfort about what
Treece saw as the growing tide of Apocalyptic or Neo-Romantic re-

bellion: "I have mentioned you as being a new member of the Apocalyptic group in an essay which Greacen asked me to write," wrote Treece, adding, "It looks as though there will be a show-down soon; Spender versus the real 'younger' poets." The larger world was also enacting a show-down of sorts. On 8 December, the Allies declared war on Japan, and on 11 December the United States declared war on Germany.

A Question of Style

Treece, Fraser, D. S. Savage, Comfort, Moore, and Gardiner have all called attention to the fact that much of the poetry, but particularly that which is antiestablishment in nature, of the 1940s is written partly in reaction to the "poets of the Auden generation," as Spender called them—W. H. Auden, C. Day Lewis, Louis MacNeice, and Spender himself.[34] It was a reaction, it may be added, that in some ways repeats the earlier nineteenth-century Romantic revolt against the more journalistic, prosaic, rational, topical, and urban-focused eighteenth-century Neo-Classicism of Dryden, Pope, and Johnson. Comfort recalls liking the fact that Treece was "getting a much greater richness of language" into his work "than we had had lately."[35] More recently, Comfort writes,

In fine, Apocalypse was a planned attempt to inject more eloquence and a more archimagical touch into poetry which had become a bit dry in the hands of our immediate predecessors—rather as one injects butter into a roasting turkey. It leaned heavily on what was in effect Bardic diction (odd that we didn't learn more from Yeats) and some of its purpler rhetoric reads very like a translation from Welsh set Bardic odes.[36]

Some of the more Romantic poets of the 1930s and 1940s reject the urban focus of much Neo-Classical poetry, including Eliot's, to give back to nature the numinosity it had for the nineteenth-century Romantics. Like Wordsworth, Thomas, Sidney Keyes, Treece, George Barker, and Watkins, while depicting nature's terrifying destructiveness, intimate some meaningful underlying reality. Treece drifts toward a sort of elemental Wordworthianism, asserting in "Pastoral," "I have learnt nothing from the marble urn / The Sparrow could not teach me." But in stark contrast is Comfort's Neo-Romanticism

based on a Hardyesque or Camusian sense of nature's indifference or
hostility.

Neo-Romantic imagery, in other respects, is often of the body. In
contrast to the Auden group's images of the city's slums, dives, or
suburbs, or of automobiles, airplanes, trains, and factories, Thomas
and Treece present images of tears, heads, faces, fingers, hairs, and
eyes; and, delving below the skin's surface, images of hearts, blood,
fetal existence, wombs, and wombs penetrated in phallic symbolism.
Skeletal imagery, in X-ray vision worthy of Baudelaire, appears more
often in Neo-Romantic poetry and functions as *memento mori*. Natural
imagery, such as rain, sea, caves, earth, and landscape, tends more
often than in poetry of the Auden group to symbolize male and female anatomy and orgasm and female receptivity. Artificial imagery,
or the imagery of human artifacts, appears in Neo-Romantic poetry,
but often as *momento mori,* as in clock imagery, or as symbols of the
body, as in sword, knife, candle, chalice, and box imagery symbolic
of male and female sexual organs.

Sir Herbert Read

Sir Herbert Read's influence on the Apocalyptic Movement was acknowledged at the outset by Treece and Fraser. As Moore has recently
noted concerning the movement, "Sir Herbert Read, of course, spon-
sored it."[37] He also influenced the larger Neo-Romanticism, and Gardiner writes that Read was "a great help in publicizing" Neo-Romanticism in his *Politics of the Unpolitical*.[38] In addition, Read's reputation
as an art critic, gained with the publication of *Reason and Romanticism*
(1926), *Phases of English Poetry* (1923), and *The Sense of Glory* (1929),
aided in legitimizing Neo-Romanticism. "With the publication of
Art Now" (1933), as noted in *Current Biography* (1962), Read "was
established as Britain's most influential writer on modern art."[39]

As Woodcock notes, Read was also helpful to Neo-Romanticism
generally by bringing out the books of many of the younger Neo-
Romantics while he was a director at Routledge & Kegan Paul.[40] He
was helpful certainly to Treece and Comfort. In a 20 May 1942 letter, Treece expresses to Comfort his delight in a recent broadcast,
presumably BBC, in which Read had "something nice to say" about
him and Comfort. More under Read's spell than Hendry, Treece to

Comfort praises Read profusely. Noting that he was with Read "the weekend he wrote" an article, Treece continues, "Alex, you must always remember this, and what is more, teach your children to say it every night; Herbert Read is a GREAT man (nothing short of that), for he is noble, humble, sensitive and strong; he knows more than any man I know the value of the heart as opposed to the head. . . ." Treece concludes, "May God strike me dead if I ever lift a finger against him, and may the devil himself take away my bowels if I allow another to say black words of him in my hearing."

T. S. Eliot. Read's association with T. S. Eliot may have helped to focus Eliot's influence upon the Apocalyptic Movement, which, as Fraser notes, tends to derive its techniques partly from Eliot.[41] Eliot met Read in the autumn of 1917, and their close personal relationship lasted until Eliot's death in 1965.[42] With Read he established the *Criterion,* which was partly derived from Read's *Art and Letters.* It was intended to be an avant-garde literary magazine furthering Eliot's objective, "a 'phalanx' whose unity would be reflected" in its pages. "I imply the formation of a party, of a 'new front,' " Read recollects, "and that was indeed the intention, as the 'commentaries' in *The Criterion* soon made clear."[43] The *Criterion*'s "new front" left its imprint on the poetry of the 1940s. Eliot's condensation of sense, Neo-Classical analyses of subjective states of mind, and reliance on a mythical mode of development seem influencial on Neo-Romanticism generally. But both Read and the later Neo-Romantics are much less self-consciously intellectual and allusive than Eliot.

T. E. Hulme's essay on "Romanticism and Classicism" is generally recognized as an important contribution to the modern Neo-Classical philosophical and aesthetic perspective. It was Read who, at Alfred Richard Orage's request, edited Hulme's posthumous papers, published as *Speculations: Essays on Humanism and the Philosophy of Art* in 1924. "I agreed," Read recollects, "not realizing (though I had often read Hulme's contributions to *The New Age*) what a bombshell I was innocently manufacturing."[44] His views had changed considerably since his first war-diary entries in January 1915, when he had just turned twenty-one. In an entry dated 6.iii.15, Read writes that "the highest expression of virtue that I know of is found in the last lines of Shelley's 'Prometheus'—emphasis being laid on Hope and Defiance."[45] But sounding very much like Hulme, Read later writes that "Romanticism is—in literature—the confusion of the human with the divine. . . . Someone described a Romantic as a person who didn't believe in the Fall of Man and Original Sin."[46] Read announced a more settled conclusion in an entry dated 25.iii.17: "I have lost the basic belief of my old pessimism—a belief in the doctrine of original sin," partly because it "implies a denial of mental evolution,"[47] which is, by implication, a part of the larger biological evolution defined by Darwin.

When Eliot asked Read to prepare a volume of essays for Faber & Gwyer, where Eliot was an editorial director, Read compiled *Reason and Romanticism* (1926). He explains: ". . . though the Reason of it owes something to Hulme and even more to Eliot, the Romanticism was my own. It was already my declared purpose to seek some reconciliation or 'synthesis' of these opposed faiths."[48]

Eliot was moving toward a different faith. At Eliot's house at Chester Terrace in London, Read, who sometimes would spend the night after "Criterion dinners," woke early on one occasion to see Eliot's "hand and then . . . arm reach round the door and lift from a hook the bowler hat that was hanging there." Eliot was "on his way to an early communion service," Read writes, adding, "It was the first intimation I had had of his conversion to the Christian faith."[49] In 1927 Eliot joined the Church of England. Read recalls that when Eliot in the preface to *For Lancelot Andrews* (1928) called himself "a classicist in literature, a royalist in politics and an anglo-catholic in religion, I could only retort that I was a romanticist in literature, an anarchist in politics and an agnostic in religion."[50] Dylan Thomas then felt obliged to announce "his independence" by calling himself "a Welshman, a drunkard, and a heterosexual."[51]

Imagism.   By 1920 Read's circle of friends also included Ezra Pound, Wyndham Lewis, the Sitwell brothers, Richard Aldington, and F. S. Flint—"they were his friends and associates, as leaders of the post war movement in English literature," Woodcock notes.[52] Stephen Spender recalls that in the 1920s what he "admired" about Eliot, Pound, Read, the Sitwells, and other modernists was partly their "hard clear imagery."[53]

As a poet, Read is essentially in the Imagist tradition, which he saw as extending into the twentieth century the "principles" of nineteenth-century Romanticism.[54] Although Richard Aldington had in

1922 attacked "Read (and others of his 'school')" for their "allusive and elliptic" style, "abstruse and ponderous" vocabulary, and "tenuous and remote" meanings, his comments apply better to Eliot's *The Waste Land* (1922) than they do to Read's poetry.[55] His "philosophy of composition" began to develop while he was a British soldier in the First World War. There was at the time, Read writes, "a general feeling . . . that some new philosophy was necessary, much as it had been necessary when Wordsworth and Coleridge published their *Lyrical Ballads* in 1798. . . ."[56]

Finding his Neo-Romanticism not antipathetic to Read's Imagism, Treece in his *Herbert Read: An Introduction to His Work by Many Hands* (1944) approvingly quotes from Read's "Night":

> The dark steep roofs chisel
> The infinity of the sky:
>
> But the white moonlit gables
> Resemble
> Still hands at prayer.[57]

Thinking perhaps of T. E. Hulme's castigation of Romantic poetry for the appearance in it of the "word infinite in every other line,"[58] as well as, perhaps, the Imagist rejection of poetry that is "blurred or indefinite," Treece adds, "If [Read's] infinity is indefinite, so is the concept that it describes; the wideness and emptiness of the sky are in that word."[59] Treece is arguing, in effect, that the subject matter determines the language of poetry and that Read's poetry is as definite as its subject allows. In some respects, much Neo-Romantic poetry, including Treece's, represents the sort of ambiguous and Shelleyan cosmic posturing that the Imagists reacted against. Yet Neo-Romanticism seems influenced by Imagism, perhaps partly as it is expressed in Read's poetry: Neo-Romanticism, like Imagism (as well as Surrealism, discussed below), emphasizes the primacy of the visual image in poetry.

G. S. Fraser in *The White Horseman* writes that Pound's use of the term "apparition" for "image" in his well-known "In a Station of the Metro" aptly describes the "sudden sense of relationship between apparently disconnected things: 'The apparition of those faces in the tube:/Petals on a wet, black bough.' "[60] He goes on to compare Pound's concept of the image with that of montage in the film. Fraser might have gone on to argue that the imagery of Apocalyptic poetry in particular and Neo-Romantic poetry in general reflects the development of the cinema in the twentieth century. Neo-Romantic poetry is cinematographic, whereas the imagery of the Imagists is more photographic, as evident in Read's Imagist "April":

> To the fresh wet fields
> and the white froth of flowers
>
> Came the wild errant
> swallows with a scream.

Neo-Romanticism generally, including the poetry of Thomas, Barker, Treece, and Hendry, reflects also the Imagist influence on modern poetry inasmuch as concentration, although not its "very essence," is in much of it an aesthetic goal.

   The Introspective Tone.   Spender recalls also admiring Read and other modernists for their "search for means of expressing complicated states of consciousness and acute sensibility."[61] Similarly impressed, Banerjee observes in his *Spirit Above Wars* that Read's "To a Conscript of 1940" "set the tone"—"introspective and ironic rather than social and hysterical"—for "the English poets who wrote about, and some of whom died in, the Second World War. . . ." In the poem, Read "encounters a soldier of the previous war who has come to the grim realization that 'Our victory was our defeat!' Thus he can help the poet to view the war, and his role in it, with a greater sense of reality."[62]

   Disillusionment with war and war heroics is the point of Read's poem. But the tone is also social, and Read's disillusionment does not negate his hope for a noncoercive society. The problem from Read's perspective is that the "world was not renewed" and cannot be renewed through military force and governmental power:

> We think we gave in vain. The world was not renewed.
>   There was hope in the homestead and anger in the streets
> But the old world was restored and we returned
>   To the dreary field and workshop, and the immemorial feud
>
> Of rich and poor. Our victory was our defeat.
>   Power was retained where power had been misused. . . .

Read's "Ode Without Rhetoric," included by Treece and Schimanski in the first *Transformation* anthology, has similar implications. Remembering his experiences as a soldier in the First World War, Read writes:

> One of the dazed and disinherited
> I crawled out of that mess
> with two medals and a gift of blood-money.
> No visible wounds to lick—only a resolve
> to tell the truth about war and about men
> involved in the indignities of war.
>
> . . . .
>
> And so we drifted twenty years
> down the stream of time
> feeling that such a storm
> could not break again
> feeling that our little house-boat was safe
> until the last lock was reached.

It is Read's amalgam of cynicism about war and power politics and optimism about the possibility of personal and social renewal which sets the tone for much of the Neo-Romantic poetry and prose of the 1940s. In his conclusion to "Ode Without Rhetoric," Read writes of the "self perfected/tranquil as a dove/the heart elected/to mutual aid"—i.e., to the principle of species solidarity discovered by the anarchist ethologist Peter Kropotkin.

The Green Child.   Read wrote only one novel, *The Green Child* (1935), which Graham Greene "would put among the great poems of this century."[63] The novel is about Olivero, who journeys to London to realize his ambitions as a writer; to South America, where in Roncador he becomes dictator; to England, where he first encountered the Green Child; and finally to her underground world, where he finds spiritual fulfillment in progressing toward a contemplative existence.

Geography functions symbolically in *The Green Child.* Olivero's descent with the Green Child, Siloën as she is now called, into the hidden recesses of the underground world symbolically suggests, among other things, the quest for identity and self-discovery involved in Jungian depth psychology. The descent into the cave was for Jung, one of Read's friends, an archetype, as his memoirs make clear. In one of Jung's "confrontations" with the unconscious, he descends into an underground world in which he meets "an old man" and a "beautiful young girl," who calls herself Salome. "Salome is an anima figure," Jung observes, and he notes as well that "in such dream wanderings one frequently encounters an old man who is accompanied by a young girl. . . ."[64] Read's wise old men of the underground world are from the same archetypal mold and represent spiritual guides. In another dream vision, Jung, "descending again," enters a "low cave cut into the rock," in which he finds the "remains of a primitive culture." Finding Freud's interpretations unsatisfactory (he finds Jung's skeletal remains suggestive of "secret death wishes"), Jung concludes that in "the cave, I discovered remains of a primitive culture, that is, the world of the primitive man within myself—a world which can scarcely be reached or illuminated by consciousness."[65] The primitivism of Read's underground beings has similar implications.

Obscure Reveries

The Eye of the Mind.   Olivero's journey away from external affairs and politics and toward inwardness prefigures the internal quests of some of the Neo-Romantics in the 1940s. The environment which Treece and Hendry argue for is largely internal. Wrey Gardiner's Neo-Romantic "Lament for Strings" expresses his analogous intentions:

> . . . Patiently we build
> These tonal structures in the architecture
> Of the dark mind, empty and alone. . . .

Gardiner's metaphoric "eye of the mind" in *The Once Loved God*[66] reflects earlier Romantic metaphoric expressions for the inward vision, such as Wordsworth's "inward eye," which is the "bliss of solitude," or Blake's "Imaginative Eye" in "A Vision of the Last Judgment." In contrast, MacNeice articulates the tendency of left-wing poets in the 1930s to focus more on the social, objective world in his defense of poets who "look . . . outwards" in his "Autumnal Journal." Like Read and Jung, the Neo-Romantics in general adopted an essentially nineteenth-century Romantic view of the sensitive artist as necessarily self-reflecting and modern society as characterized by an appalling lack of introspection.

Moreover, the perception that external reality was becoming increasingly intolerable was undoubtedly a cause as well of the renewed emphasis on individual perspective and subjectivity in poetry generally during the 1930s and 1940s. In an external environment in which the individual was increasingly insignificant in contrast to seemingly larger-than-life leaders or heroes (Hitler, Mussolini, Hirohito, Churchill, and Roosevelt), Kenneth Patchen and Treece in effect elevated the poet-prophet as hero, a revived Shelleyian unacknowledged legislator of the world. In an external social and political landscape increasingly barren, Treece, Hendry, David Gascoyne, and Gardiner emphasize the development of a compensatory rich inner life less limited by the seeming impoverishing reality principle. In a world moving toward war and less personal freedom, such poets retreat—or, more from their point of view, advance—into an internal citadel of the mind in which time, externally limited by war, could be stretched and bent, like Salvador Dali's timepieces, and in which solid objects, in contrast to increasingly intractable institutions and events, became malleable or plastic.

The highly subjective style of some Neo-Romantics also reflects their growing alienation from modern mass culture, which utilizes language, as Orwell, Huxley, and Jaspers suggest, not to raise consciousness, a traditionally Romantic objective, but to inculcate the collectivist objectives of the dominant culture. Reacting also to the objectification of the individual and human experience in the natural sciences and Watsonian behaviorism, which excludes from discourse the products of introspection, such Neo-Romantics assert the poet's mind to be a sufficient and unlimited reservoir of material. Fraser articulates the Apocalyptic position: ". . . every poet has enough to write about in the contents of his own mind. . . ."[67] Similarly influenced by depth psychology, Norman MacCaig in *Far Cry* (1943) writes of the "hidden person, the fathomless difficult being/that bridges us together as a single animal. . . ."[68] Such a perspective recalls Hulme's astute definition of Romanticism in "Romanticism and Classicism": "Here is the root of all romanticism: that man, the individual, is an infinite reservoir of possibilities. . . ."[69]

Therapeutic Art. A correlate assumption that influences the

works of poets such as Lawrence, Supervielle, Patchen, Thomas, John
Bayliss, Barker, and Treece is that exposure of the unconscious in art
has a psychotherapeutic value similar to that gained through Freudian
or Jungian psychoanalysis. Freud's emphasis on the psychopathology
of everyday experience virtually guaranteed that psychoanalytically
directed writers would view the poetry-making process as one way of
exorcising the internal demons of supposedly ubiquitous mental ill-
ness. Nightmarish imagery in Apocalyptic and Neo-Romantic poetry
generally superficially suggests that such demons have at least been
detected if not cast out.

Consequently, Fraser in "Apocalypse in Poetry" in *The White
Horseman* can argue that "if the poetry of the Auden generation had
a certain immediate political and social value, the poetry of the Apocalyptics is likely to have a certain permanent clinical value for the
human species."[70] Such aesthetic theories connect with earlier Romantic assumptions about the cathartic function of poetry. Barker,
like Genet, eventually comes to engage in confessional art in which
private, autobiographical material is blatantly revealed. Most Neo-
Romantics in the 1940s, however, from lack of experience or inhibi-
tions, engage less in explicit revelations of private, intimate behavior.

Surrealism.   Such aesthetic theories are also a product of Surrealism's influence upon Neo-Romanticism. Hendry has noted that he
attended the Surrealist exhibition in London in 1936.[71] It "caused a
minor scandal."[72] Salvador Dali lectured but was "inaudible" because
he was wearing "a diver's helmet."[73] André "Breton attended the
opening with Mme. Breton, who had blue hair." "Crowded with
friends and acquaintances," Thomas "carried a cup of boiled string
around. 'Weak or strong?' he asked, offering it to . . . . Breton, Sir
Herbert Read, and the buffoons of the unconscious," according to
Tindall.[74] Read edited *Surrealism* (1936), an anthology accompanying
the exhibition and the " 'definitive manifesto' of the British group."[75]
Surrealism, which contained Read's "Surrealism and the Romantic
Principle," helped to popularize Surrealism in England. And as Morgan notes in *A New Romantic Anthology* (1949), it was "largely
through Herbert Read's instrumentality" that Surrealism "began to
be potent in English literary circles. . . ."[76] The Apocalyptic Movement both Treece and Fraser agree "derives from Surrealism," em-
bodying "what is positive in Surrealism, 'the effort,' in Herbert

Read's phrase, 'to realize some of the dimensions and characteristics of man's submerged being.' "[77]

George Orwell in "The Dark Horse of the Apocalypse," a review of *The New Apocalypse* and Treece's *Thirty-Eight Poems* (1940), concludes that the "main enemy" of the "Apocalyptic group" "is the group most closely akin to them, the Surrealists. The objects of the movement are set forth in J. F. Hendry's introduction . . . and it would seem that what is being aimed at is (approximately) Surrealism with the brake on."[78] The "main enemy" was not Surrealism. But Treece, Hendry, and Fraser do argue for a consciously controlled form of Surrealism. In "Apocalypse in Poetry" Fraser writes that the New Apocalypse is what one might call "a dialectical development" of Surrealism, the "next stage forward." Unlike Surrealism, the New Apocalypse "insists on the reality of the conscious mind, as an independent formative principle. . . ."[79] In this respect, Gascoyne's development beyond Surrealism is similar: ". . . I found that automatic writing was no longer satisfactory. I wanted to—I had to allow the conscious element and molding and making to play a part."[80]

Surrealism also influenced Neo-Romantics like Comfort, Gardiner, Derek Stanford, and John Bayliss, whose "Seven Dreams" reads almost as a series of frames of Surrealist paintings. (Bayliss was influenced also by Hugh Sykes Davies, one of his supervisors at Cambridge, who wrote the first Surrealist novel in England, *Petron*, 1935.)[81] Intensifying the influence of nineteenth-century Romanticism, the Surrealist influence allowed in theory a greater passivity and spontaneity in the creative process on the part of Neo-Romantic poets, as compared to Auden-generation poets and Neo-Classicists, such as Hulme and Eliot. But the automatism of André Breton and André Masson and the seemingly nonsensical and illogical, but often analogical, style of much of the poetry of Gascoyne, Barker, and Thomas quickly becomes a matter of imitation and conscious planning, like Thomas's boiled cup of string and Mme Breton's blue hair.

The Fauna of the Mind. Yet it might be argued that some inwardly focused Neo-Romantics, like some religious visionaries, gain their imagery and obsessions partly from the unconscious and its recurring archetypes, as Jung or Read would call them. Carl Sagan advances in his *The Dragons of Eden* hypotheses which may help to explain the preoccupation in Romantic and Neo-Romantic literature, as well as in religious mythologies, with Eden (or the Golden Age), the fall from Eden into an awareness of individuality and death, darkness and night, and the dragon or serpent as archetypal foe. Sagan argues,

Perhaps the Garden of Eden is not so different from Earth as it appeared to our ancestors of some three or four million years ago, during a legendary golden age when the genus *Homo* was perfectly interwoven with the other beasts and vegetables.

. . . .

One of the earliest consequences of the anticipatory skills that accompanied the evolution of the prefrontal lobes must have been the awareness of death. . . . It is not that death was absent before the spectacular growth of the neocortex, before the exile from Eden; it is only that, until then, no one had ever noticed that death would be his destiny.

. . . .

After the extinction of the dinosaurs, mammals moved into daytime ecological niches. The primate fear of the dark must be a comparatively recent development. Washburn has reported that infant baboons and other young primates appear to be born with only three inborn fears—of falling, snakes, and the dark—corresponding respectively to the dangers posed by Newtonian gravitation to tree-dwellers, by our ancient enemies the reptiles. . . .[82]

The "mutual hostility between man and dragon" is "a worldwide phenomenon," Sagan also observes; he goes on to give the St. George and the dragon myth as one example.[83] Literature students would want to include Beowulf and Grendel as another.

Such bizarre but imaginative conclusions may also help to explain a curious facet of apocalyptic mentality. To elicit fear and trembling, intimate terrifying destructiveness (a typical part of apocalyptic visions), or symbolize the forces of evil and death, some apocalyptic writers use images of dragons (dim "memories" of dinosaurs, Sagan would argue) or beasts. St. John's Revelation contains a "great red dragon"[84] and a beast that rises out of the sea[85] and anticipates as well the final "victory over the beast, and over his image. . . ."[86]

A beast is also linked with an awesome recycling of the historical process in Yeats's apocalyptic "The Second Coming." The cinema since the 1950s, in which apocalyptic anxieties, most associated with the possibility of a nuclear holocaust, are expressed indirectly through images of beasts or monsters, as some would argue, provides additional examples.

Serpents are also Jungian archetypes. In his *Memories, Dreams, Reflections* (1961), Jung records a dream vision containing "a black serpent," which he notes is frequently a mythical "counterpart of the hero," and its presence in dream visions is "an indication of the hero-myth."[87] Such an interpretation may be applicable to Treece's *The Ballad of the Prince*, which reflects St. John's presentation of Christ the "prince"[88] and heroic destroyer of the serpent, Lucifer. Treece, alluding to the "bottomless pit" into which "the dragon, that old serpent, which is the Devil" is cast,[89] writes in his "Prologue," "heere shal bee Darkness of the Pit and no Light; the Sepulchre but no Floweres; the Serpent but no maner of Delight." But in "Poem" (beginning "When Spring's caress"), Treece presents the poet-prophet as a hero, who, like St. George, dares "the dragon's wrath":

> What man has done and lived to tell the world
> I'll do again. I'll dare the dragon's wrath
> And in the company of angels bawl the word
> That baffles oracles, makes dead bones ring. . . .

Taming in fantasy the ancient antagonist, or, better yet, turning it into a friend and protector rather than an enemy and destroyer, is in Treece's "Y Ddraig Goch" a desirable prerogative of childhood dreams and reverie. Apparently finding St. John's "great" "red dragon" inspirational, Treece writes,

> The dragon of our dreams roared in the hills
> That ring the sunlit land of children's songs.
> Red with the lacquer of a fairy-tale,
> His fiery breath fried all beseiging knights.
>
> Whole seasons could he lay the land in waste
> By huffing once upon the standing corn!
> He was our dragon dressed in red, who kept
> Sly ghosts from lurking underneath the thatch. . . .

The tone of "Y Ddraig Goch" is similar to that of Barrie's *Peter Pan*. The poem concludes, "Don't die, old dragon, wait a few years more,/ I shall come back and bring you boys to love."

But archetypal interpretations are lopsided if they imply, as they sometimes do, that poetic or religious imagery and themes are predominantly the product of an innate collective unconscious. Rather, such imagery as it appears in Neo-Romantic poetry, as well as in modern art generally, seems predominantly the product of conscious or unconscious reworking and reorganizing of personal memories and the imagery and themes of earlier religious and literary models, or as archetypes, dim cultural memories rather than in-built species "memories."

Chapter Two

James F. Hendry: Apocalyptic Poet and Apologist

Apocalypse

Confusion about the meaning of the term *apocalypse* began at the out-set of the Apocalyptic Movement and plagues subsequent interpretations. Consequently, Dylan Thomas in 1938 can write to John Goodland that although he has not yet seen the Apocalyptic "manifesto," ". . . many of your suggested contributors [to the first Apocalyptic anthology] are, I am certain, by any definition, among the least apocalyptic writers alive. . . ."[1] And Nicholas Moore, one of the brightest poets associated with the Apocalyptic Movement, can write in 1980: "One of my troubles with Apocalypse and apocalyptic is that I have never known exactly what it means."[2]

Literary critics have generally avoided defining the term *apocalypse,* while sometimes discussing what they believe to be the salient features of the philosophy of the Apocalyptic Movement. Finding "irrationalism" a dominant motif, Hoffman emphasizes that the "young English poets of the early 1940s, who called themselves the poets of 'The New Apocalypse,' had been introduced to Freud and to the surrealists quite early in their careers."[3] To explain the Apocalyptic Movement, Hoffman, Helmstadter, and Francis Scarfe (in *Auden and After,* 1942) reproduce and discuss Hendry's 1938 Apocalyptic "manifesto." But they leave unexplained the significance of the term *apocalypse* to either the Apocalyptic Movement or art generally in the 1930s and 1940s. Jo Ann Baggerly, however, drawing from David Erdman's edition of *The Poetry and Prose of William Blake,* is willing to venture, without significant development of the definition, that "an Apocalyptic poet" is "any poet adhering concurrently to a deep belief in the decadence of the world, a prophetic confidence of its renovation, and the conviction that his age is the transitional period between the two."[4] Such a definition does in fact apply, although Baggerly errs in both limiting the definition to this meaning and to the Apocalyptic Movement. St. John's apocalyptic vision in Revelation of course provides a model. St. John sees the end of one age and the beginning of another. Yeats's "The Second Coming" is apocalyptic in this sense and presumably also provides a popular model for subsequent apocalyptic poetry. Forcibly dramatizing the Marxist aspirations of the 1930s, Odets's *Awake and Sing!* is also in this sense apocalyptic.

Answering a question on how the Apocalyptic poets were "misunderstood by the general public and reviewers," James F. Hendry notes that they were perceived as "wild and incoherent—'last-judgment'—preachers."[5] Such misinterpretations are not surprising, since the poetry of the Apocalyptic Movement does contain end-of-the-world imagery. It sometimes reflects, in this sense, the popular imagination in which *apocalypse* often implies end-of-the-world catastrophic destruction, not always attended by renovation. Again, St. John's Apocalypse provides a model. In his *Apocalypse* (1931), D. H. Lawrence argues that St. John's Apocalypse is divided "into two halves, with two rather discordant intentions." Lawrence adds that the first half appears to leave the world "renewed." But the "apocalyptist" in the second half envisions the "end of the world" and *"must* see the universe . . . wiped out utterly, and merely a heavenly city and a hellish lake of brimstone left."[6] The conflict between the two parts, it may be added, reflects in part the unstable New-Testament combination, as Albert Schweitzer was the first to realize fully, of traditional Jewish eschatological aspirations for the fulfillment of Old-Testament prophecies about the establishment in this world of the Messianic kingdom and, on the other hand, newer concepts, incorporated into the New Testament, of hell, demons, and an otherworldly heaven. In the twentieth century also the meaning of *apocalypse* is ambiguous and confusing partly because it reflects such divergent ideas at work in early Christian eschatology.

But end-of-the-world imagery in the poetry of the Apocalyptic Movement also reflects the developing doomsday atmosphere of the 1930s. Stephen Spender records a widespread feeling during the 1930s that "the approaching war" meant "the end of civilization," the "total destruction of all major built-up areas."[7] End-of-the-world imagery colors some of Spender's poetry, as well as that of Barker and the Surrealists. Sounding much like Spender, André Breton in his 1946 "Advertisement" for his new edition of the *Second Manifeste Du Surréalisme* notes that by 1930 a few perceptive thinkers began to realize the impending and unavoidable (or *inéluctable*) recurrence of world catastrophe (*la catastrophe mondiale*).[8]

The sense of impending doom which characterizes the eschatological sayings of Christ and New-Testament apolcalyptic mentality generally is repeated in later apocalyptic literature (Wordsworth's apocalyptic deluge in *The Prelude,* for example, is "now at hand").[9] And in the 1930s and 1940s it coalesces with—or provides convenient metaphors for—Breton's awareness of impending catastrophe and with an almost Heideggerian awareness that one may die at any moment, as in the art of Thomas, Gascoyne, Ramuz, Unamuno, and Rilke. Some of Eliot's poetry, such as "The Hollow Men" (and its well-known image of the way the world ends), provides an example, as well as a model for other poets, such as Treece. Kafka's works, such as *The Trial* and *A Country Doctor,* also contribute to the atmosphere of impending doom at work in the art of Hendry, Cooke, and Treece. Dramatically such awareness also becomes externalized into the waiting motifs of Beckett and Pinter. In Neo-Romantic poetry it is more often expressed symbolically, as in Thomas's nature imagery, and, borrowing from its New-Testament and nineteenth-century apocalyptic models, is sometimes linked with a sense of impending judgment.

The origin of the label *apocalypse* for the Apocalyptic Movement has been a subject of misunderstanding and controversy. On being asked what was his "connection" with the Apocalyptic Movement, Barker replied, "It was simply that I was the first chap who had the gumption to use the word 'apocalypse,' that was all."[10] Barker claims to have used the term "about two years before the war" in a "bit of prose somewhere or other about how nature seems to have become apocalyptic," and ". . . suddenly the word 'apocalypse' entered the language."[11] The term for the group *may* have originated with Goodland, Cooke, or Treece (but not with Moore), as Moore has acknowledged.[12] But Hendry with a good deal more assurance notes that it was he who selected the term *apocalypse,* and he did so from Lawrence's *Apocalypse* and the Bible.[13]

Confusion in literary criticism about the implications of the term *apocalypse* stems in part from the relative absence from Hendry's philosophy of end-of-the-world thinking. No *literal* analysis of Hendry's ideas or "manifesto," which were paraphrased and elaborated upon in the 1940s by Fraser and Treece, provides an explanation. Nor is the answer to be found in the framework of Freudian psychoanalysis in which both the New Apocalypse and Surrealism are embedded.

Apocalypticism, Existentialism, and Surrealism all reflect a common underlying condition: the universal collapse of traditional values in the modern period. Apocalyptic visions depict catastrophic disruptions in society. Consequently, they may be used as vehicles in art to express symbolically the catastrophic breakdown of traditional values. There are precedents. Nietzsche's madman in *Joyful Wisdom*, projecting his awareness of anomic disintegration into the universe, asks, "Who gave us the sponge to wipe away the whole horizon? What did we do when we loosened this earth from its sun?"[14] Yeats uses the Christian apocalypse in his "The Second Coming" similarly to express the collapse of traditional values, although obviously the biblical apocalypse functions as well to suggest his own sense of an apocalyptic change in the historical process. Such observations resulted in the following questions to Hendry: "Was the visionary book of Revelation's image of the end of the world functioning [for you] as a kind of metaphor for social collapse?" He answered, "Yes. Exactly. It was. It was."[15]

Anomic Disintegration

The term *apocalypse,* metaphorically interpreted, identifies the central element in Hendry's Apocalyptic philosophy. Hendry notes that the "new element" introduced into Neo-Romanticism by Apocalyptism was the awareness of "all the classic values just disappearing."[16] In the late 1930s, there seemed to be developing a new dimension to the anomic disintegration of society. Emerging from the widespread moral vacuum, Fascist idealism, as in Hitler's *Mein Kampf,* began to skip beyond even Nietzsche's notions of good and evil.

The disappearance of absolute values leads to the dizzying, depressing, terrifying, or comic conclusion that everything is possible in the art of Dostoevsky, Sartre, Barth, and Murdoch. But the collapse of traditional values may also lead to visionary ecstasy about new possibilities suddenly opening up, as in Nietzsche. Neo-Romantic writers tend to be less joyful than Nietzsche, but less regretful and anguished than Sartre, perhaps partly because Neo-Romanticism is more directly linked with nineteenth-century Romanticism. Both Romanticism and Neo-Romanticism express the positive aspects of anomie: a benign relativism in which highly individual perspectives, rather than a generally agreed upon world view, and diversity rather than uniformity, are, at least in theory, prized and cultivated.

Myth. Hendry's emphasis on private myth may be interpreted from such a perspective. Where Existentialists in the manner of Kierkegaard emphasize private, subjective truth in opposition to the truth or untruth of mass society and Hegelian rationalism, Hendry emphasizes personal myth in opposition to "socially imposed" "public myth."[17] Personal myth for Hendry inhibits or undercuts external control or manipulation by the corporate myths of society or the state. Hendry and other Neo-Romantics write in reaction to the collectivist myths of the 1930s and 1940s: the German myth of the "super race," and, as Hendry has acknowledged, "the 'New Romans' [of Mussolini], 'Soviet Man' [the Leninist-Stalinist myth], etc."[18]

As the concept is used by Hendry, myth expresses a sense of futurity, behavior shaped by the pull of the future, so to speak, instead of determined by the events of the past. Freudianism and Watsonian Behaviorism both assume that the individual's motivations are explicable from a knowledge of his past history. The emphasis on futurity in Existentialism is similar, although Sartre, in particular, while emphasizing the individual's capacity to transcend the actual, would never define the individual as potentiality but, as he makes clear, through actual accomplishment. Romanticism had earlier emphasized the possible rather than the actual, but often, also, the unbridgeable gap between human aspirations and intractable reality. Like Godwin, Shelley, Read, and other anarchist Romantics, Hendry is more optimistic. Personal myth is in part realizable.

Kafka's Influence

Hendry's "Chrysalis," a short story included in *The White Horseman,* seems written in partial imitation of Kafka's *The Metamorphosis.* The opening paragraph recalls Kafka's Gregor Samsa, metamorphosed into an insect, forced to run from his father's threatening walking stick:

Horror-agog and frog-eyed, Mrs. Greig appeared at an open door . . . with
upraised broom. David ran and ran.[19]

   Answering a question about Kafka's apparent influence on "Chrysalis," Hendry agrees, "It is true. Yes." But he adds, "Then, of
course, I was very concerned with Fascist atrocities in Italy, and so
on, at that time, which—the story seems to imply that these are real
things that happened, but the [boy's] fantasies and visions were Kafkaesque. In other words the atrocities created the Kafkaesque fantasies."[20]
   Hendry argues that "Kafka was a real prophet, and he saw these
things [Fascist atrocities] before they happened." But Kafka is also
Apocalyptic in Hendry's fundamental meaning of the term *apocalyptic,*
for Kafka foresaw future atrocities as aspects of the coming anomic
breakdown of all values: "I think he had what we would call Apocalyptic vision in the sense that he saw actual pictures from the breakdown of society. And he saw the actual atrocities being
committed. . . . He didn't know he was prophesying. He *saw* these
things. And so it partly ties up with the Apocalyptic images. But,
also, if one considers modern theories about time, you could say,
well, he managed to be able to see the future as we can see the past."
Precognition?

Precognition. Yes. Something like that. It may have had that in it. But
Dunne considers time is like a river, and we are moving along one aspect of
it. When we are asleep and have dreams and images we are able to make
contact with other—with past time and future time, you see. . . . Kafka
manages to project himself into—into the future and see what it was like.[21]

Kafka's influence on Neo-Romanticism generally is immense, although most Neo-Romantics do not view Kafka as a visionary who
actually sees the future. But there is general implicit agreement
among the Neo-Romantics and a number of other writers of the late
1930s and 1940s that Kafka's visions express the present nightmare
of violent and impersonal mass society which dehumanizes and alien-
ates its members.

Poetry

   Theodora and *The Orchestral Mountain.* The meaning of
much of Hendry's art lies in the love affair of Hendry and Theodora,

his wife. Hendry found her capable of the sort of prevision which he attributes to Kafka. During a visit to Scotland, she told a friend that her husband would be lost with his ship and return in about three months. "He was," Hendry affirms, adding, "in the period specified he did return." Such previsionary occurrences, Hendry writes, are

an aspect of Dee new to me, and apparently considerably developed since her accident. To me it is definitely prevision. But it means much more.

Dee was what is known as "sensible," not pyschic, but very sincerely interested in alleviating misfortune.[22]

Hendry found Theodora in other respects also quite remarkable: "No man or woman I have met, in life or in books, for example, lives more organically than my wife," Hendry observes in his unpublished personal wartime "Journal."[23]

In his first "Journal" entry, Hendry writes, "To-day I joined the Army, never having known service before." It was 15 November 1941. His son, David, whom he treats in "Portrait of David," a poem, was sent to Scotland to stay with Hendry's parents. Theodora remained in London. Separated from her, Hendry reflects on their meaning to each other:

She has shared everything with me: . . . mortal risks in different countries, seen and unseen, the bomb and the terror. I, who have seen her knit in a shelter, I suddenly pray when High Explosive whistled directly above and burst with a crash, only to resume her knitting immediately afterwards, although shaken, how can I ever forget her? Since the terrible beginning of the "blitz" she had elected to remain in Central London, and still lives there alone. . . .

I remember how the declaration of war found us both by sheer chance, in a London church together and how the first air-raid warning wailed immediately afterwards. We knelt together, expecting what Guernica had been given, hell-fire, death and ashes. Every moment seemed glass, as we waited for the planes. A woman fainted. I think we prayed, aware of [the] . . . terror overhead, and each other."[24]

On 27 December, Hendry writes with enthusiasm: "My wife is coming to see me next week-end. How she has endured the 'Blitz' I cannot understand." Triumphantly, in his 4 January entry, Hendry records: "Dee came to-day. All morning I had been thinking of nothing else but our meeting. I dressed in my best. . . ." On 27 February,

Hendry recalls seeing "Dee's face" at the station as she saw him off.
But in April, Hendry dutifully records, "My wife is dead."[25] On 28
March 1941, she had died in London during the Blitz.

"They told me she had died," Dorian Cooke writes later in a
"Poem in Memory of Theodora Hendry," adding, "O, let me shake
awake the mortal storm,/The frozen berries, the white/Still drops of
light." Theodora, an intelligent, sensitive woman from Gorizia (later
called Austria) who spoke English, Italian, Slovene, German, and
French, was not easily forgotten. Hendry's title poem of *The Bombed
Happiness* (1942) is rather literally about his happiness in marriage
that was bombed.

Prevision and other psychic occurrences surrounded Theodora's
death, according to Hendry's "Journal." "I knew of her death before
I was told," Hendry writes. On a train to London, he had a "strange
dream of Dee in which she was comforting" him. But "other things,
more wonderful have happened," Hendry records: "One night, as I
was going to sleep I heard her voice outside, quite clearly, call
'Jimmy!' I sat up. That was all: but I know it was unmistakable."
Later, Hendry records that Theordora again "appeared in a dream,"
"hatless" and "happy and laughing." "For such dreams," Hendry
adds, "I can see now no adequate explanation in any terminology.
The narration was always from her; not from me. I was the recipient,
the bewildered one, not she."[26]

Like the grief-stricken narrator of *The Pearl,* Hendry records visionary dreams which engender an elegiac poem. The "night of her
death," Hendry writes,

I spent in Paddington station on a wooden slab. The discomfort eased my
mind of its tension. The second night I had what can only be described as
an "electric" dream. I dreamt a poem, the most perfect I have made, but as
each word came, it was live and hung suspended in the air—word after word
and line after line. It seemed the answer to everything, and Dee or someone
was communicating it. So lovely was it, I thought it an elegy of
Rilke's. . . .[27]

On 27 October he writes, "I still miss Dee. . . ." But he determines to go on living "by an effort of will, and only to accomplish
something for her sake; perhaps to write a series of Elegies worthy of

her." Yet the composition of the elegies "is intensely difficult." While the "Germans are 35 miles from Moscow" in a battle which Hendry perceptively concludes may determine "the length of the war," he records his "compulsion" in writing the elegies. And in language prefiguring the wording of his *The Orchestral Mountain: A Symphonic Elegy,* Hendry writes, "I shall soon discover a new music, new utterance. . . ." He finds consolation in the fact that "Rilke wrote nothing for ten years, and then came the . . . Elegies, suddenly. Perhaps I believe in something of the sort. At any rate I have seen my Elegies in a dream."[28]

Like Rilke's *Duino Elegies,* in other words, Hendry sees his *Orchestral Mountain* as visionary, elicited in parts while the poet is in a comparatively passive state, and inwardly focused.

In *The Penguin Book of Scottish Short Stories,* which he edited, Hendry includes his "The Caves of Altamira." It is a moving, partly autobiographical account of a couple caught in London during the Blitz. About the story, Treece in a 16 January 1944 letter to Hendry writes, "Stefan [Schimanski] showed me your story, *The Catacomb* [an earlier title to the same story] . . . the other week. Jim, it is great, and I'm not ashamed to tell you it brought me to tears." Treece adds,

I wanted it printed as much as a memorial as a piece of wonderful writing, and asked Stefan to use it. He agreed with me, and is very enthusiastic about it. Jim, you have suffered, God alone knows. I realise how much as time goes on. But you are strong now; you are stronger than you ever were before.[29]

In the story, the narrator's "world had come to an end—in the Catacomb of Love"—a symbol fusing underground air-raid shelters and Theodora's labyrinthian and disturbed mental processes. The medical certificate gave her cause of death as (1) "myocardial degeneration" and, as "a secondary and subsidiary cause," (2) " 'exhaustion of mania.' "[30] This diagnosis, Hendry notes, "seems in accord with events, the result of blast, and her subsequent attempt to fight it without understanding anything except that she felt a mortal process was going on."[31] *The Orchestral Mountain*'s final image of "the marriage of the mad girl caged in hope,/Dead as a song-bird in the naked rains" refers to Theodora.

Hendry begins his story with his narrator's frantic and useless evo-
cation: " 'Dee!' " The opening of the second elegy of *The Orchestral
Mountain* expresses a similar poignant reaction to Theodora's death.
But Dee is now Persephone, who in the myth frustrates a grief-
stricken Demeter after her abduction by Pluto to Hades:

"Persephone! Persephone!"
Her fingers break me a star and the seabirds.
They break me the moon in icy coins,

Violins sawn through, sawdust words
Awash in the tides of the underworld,

And, littered with stones of suicide, towns
Are waves they break along a wild seaboard.
Our time is shorn. Days huddle sheaves.
The wind is a broken sky of leaves.

In the broken city, still in a gale,
The broken heart is a broken jail,

Breaking from dark subconscious earth
A river of leaves whispering the sun

"Persephone! Persephone!"

It is the poet's heartfelt grief that has become obsessional or inescapable, like a "jail," and his "broken city" is London caught in a destructive, fiery "gale" as a result of the bombing. References to a
"dark subconscious earth" suggest the grave and recall Lawrence's use
of the underworld to which Persephone journeys in "Bavarian Gentians" as a metaphor for the Freudian unconscious.

In his third elegy, Hendry contrasts "Park" and city to find, as do
other Romantics, the city inferior: from his elegiac point of view, inferior because thanatotic citizens "have forgotten in the city" the reality of immortality implied by the natural, cyclical renewal in the
"Park" or nature. But the "broken city" functions also as a metaphor
expressing the anomic disintegration of Western civilization. Its implied opposite, to be developed later in the poem, is an unbroken or

whole city representing both spiritual wholeness and a promise of immortality in the city of God.

Hendry ends his fifth elegy with a question about immortality directed to "Eurydike": "Planted in the dust were we/Enchanted ghosts, Eurydike?" Theordora thus becomes Eurydice. Hendry's comparison is apt. In the myth, it is Orpheus, like Demeter earlier yearning for Persephone, who follows Eurydice to Pluto's underground world. Hendry has partly in mind his own marital bliss with Theodora in choosing the myth of Orpheus, who was blissfully married to Eurydice when she was suddenly abducted by Pluto. But the Orpheus comparison, which appears later in the poem, allows as well Hendry to identify implicitly with the mythical Orpheus, the poet and musician, who makes his own symphonic elegy, in Hendry's language, to charm Pluto and Persephone into releasing Eurydice from the underworld or death.

Furthermore, Hendry's Eurydice comparison allows an additional comparison of Theodora and Lot's wife:

> Wing her now across our former distances
> O gods of marble in the gardens! Forge
> Her in the hours of your white silence
> Hovering on the verge of speech submerged.
>
> What say they, these breasts of alabaster?
> "Looking back my lot is stricken stone."
> "I was frightened by a faun."
> "Moods are maenads I must master."

Hendry's pun combines fate, as in "my lot in life"; his identification with Lot, whose wife was turned into a pillar of salt—the imagery fuses marble cemetery statues and alabaster saints reminding the poet of Lot's wife—for "looking back" at fire-bombed (Genesis 19:24) Sodom and Gomorrah; and Hendry's own backward gaze as elegist. Moreover, mythical Orpheus, like Lot, promises not to look back when leading Eurydice out of Hell, which is implicitly associated here with fire-bombed London and Sodom and Gomorrah.

Hendry finally arrives at his orchestral mountain in the elegy beginning "Let us break into blue music, like the sea,/This hour-glass

shivering at the wind's note./Let us blossom, Sirius, on shores no eye
may see. . . ." Such imagery emphasizes that the world Hendry is
exploring is internal. Treece's imagery of "a land no eye has seen" in
"Mystic Numbers" works similarly.

In "Golgotha," Hendry, joining the sense of sight with chronological awareness, writes of "An eye of time . . . blinded by this bone,"
itself a seen *memento mori* of time passing. Practicing a kind of Bau-
delairean synaesthesia, Hendry similarly describes "blue music." But
his unrealistic descriptions also recall Breton's Surrealistic poetry, as
in "Tiki," in which Breton's egg in a simile is red or green rather
than white ("Je t'aime à la face des mers/Rouge comme l'oeuf quand
il est vert. . . ."). Such Surrealistic qualities contribute to the diffi-
culty readers have understanding Hendry's poetry. Concerning stanza
four, which presents the core of Hendry's vision of the mountain,
Helmstadter writes, "Now that we have arrived at the mountain,
what is the myth of vision that may be seen? It would be very hard
to apply a logical or rational equivalent to such a stanza. . . ."[32]
Stanza four reads,

> There I have heard the rich sound of gold in ore
> In the side of a mountain shrill with fluted silver.
> I have listened where glaciers slow as waxen tears
> Flow down all the wild honey of the years.
> I have seen the spirit starred in a grain of dust:
> In waves of sleep, black from the hidden sun, blown
> Pollen of eternity, death's rust
> Seeded in sorrow, the flower of the psyche grown,
> August admiral of beauty, anchored for ascension
> Beneath the Mountain, history's apex, the crucifixion.[33]

In these lines, according to Helmstadter, Hendry's "vision becomes
universal as, in Dylan Thomas fashion, he imaginatively goes down
the wild honey years to the beginning of life and sees it as one whole.
The mystery and excitement of the vision rather than its nature are
being communicated here."[34]

For Hendry, the numinosity of his visionary experience may be
protected by being beyond rational analysis. Irrational associations, as
in Surrealist poetry, are, in any case, detectable. "Wild honey" is associated with "Pollen of eternity" in the poem, and, biblically, with

the prophet-seer John the Baptist, who fed on wild honey. Both symphonic mountain and "wild honey" also recall Coleridge's dream vision "Kubla Khan" in which an "abyssinian maid" sings of "Mount Abora" and an inspired poet-seer has fed on "honey-dew" and "drunk the milk of Paradise."

Hendry's allusion to Christ's "crucifixion," on a "Mountain," a variation of the biblical hill called Golgotha, suggests the redemptive myth of Christianity is both "history's apex" and becoming an integral part of Hendry's private myth, his symphonic mountain. Wholeness of vision seems implied by Hendry's associational linking of disparate aspects of experience, as well as by his having "seen the spirit starred in a grain of dust," a line recalling the visionary Blake, who could "see a World in a grain of sand."

In concluding this elegy, Hendry writes:

> Yet every stone is there, each one with a voice.
> Sapphire justice, wisdom's emerald, the opal of pity.
> As they live and breathe the loud song of their choice.
> Angelic clamour fascinates this city.
> Joyous ruby and the steadfast turquoise hold
> Colours of flower and star in a heaven of cold,
> In a haven of seas that break only into sky.
> Deep as deluged ice in a shaft and fountain
> Stream their sleepless suns through every tired mind's eye
> And crown with coronas of lightning the Orchestral Mountain.

In stanza one, Hendry had written of "wishes" that "Shall marshal chaotic mutiny into a chord," and it is to the notion of harmony that Hendry returns in his final stanza. The apparently circular or cone-shaped mountain recalls Jung's mandalas, which are symbolic of psychic wholeness and self-realization. The mandala symbolism of Hendry's mountain is intensified by his vision of the "coronas of lightning" which "crown" the Orchestral Mountain. Ascension of the mountain, which is "anchored for ascension," suggests the poet-pilgrim's upward journey toward Theodora and completion. "Live and breathe" is a transformed cliché ("as I live and breathe"); but stones acquiring life and "the loud song of their choice" recall Christ's triumphal entry into the holy city of Jerusalem.[35]

Hendry's "city" suggests the redemption of the "broken city" of

the second elegy and of the mechanized, urbanized environment
which Hendry, Treece, and Fraser find dehumanizing. Mythically,
Hendry leaves Dante's Inferno or Bunyan's city of destruction (which,
Christian informs his family, "will be burned with fire from
heaven"[36]) to experience purgation and discover inward salvation
while pilgrimaging through a European wasteland being devastated
by war. In such a mythical context, Hendry's mountain and heavenly
city, with its "Angelic clamour," is a version of the goal of Bunyan's
pilgrim, led by his guides, "the Shining Ones": "There, said they, is
the Mount Zion, the heavenly Jerusalem, the innumerable company
of angels, and the spirits of just men made perfect."[37] But Bunyan's
extended dream vision is itself based on St. John's vision of Mount
Zion upon which the redeemed stand and sing "as it were a new
song," having escaped Babylon, "that great city," which, announces
an angel, "is fallen. . . ."[38] Mountains are also biblical symbols associated with revelation and prophecy, Moses's and Christ's, or apocalyptic inspiration, as in Coleridge's "Mount Abora" or in Barker's
"Holy Poems."

The following elegy sheds more light on the cosmic imagery of
Hendry's mountain. His "conceit," or exaggerated and elaborate metaphor of the mountain, and associated imagery, Hendry now views as
a catharsis for his grief over Theodora's death:

> If now I wept again, even stars and pearls,
> It were only conceit's catharsis. None of these
> Would weave a tiara around the universe
> Or scatter light among the seven seas.
> This grief is grace to shed.

Thomas, in his elegiac "After the Funeral," provides a similar explanation for his exaggerated cosmic conceit (Ann's "hooded, fountain
heart once fell in puddles/. . . and drowned each sun") used to express his grief over Ann's death: ". . . this for her is monstrous image
blindly/magnified out of praise; her death was a still drop. . . ."

In *The White Horseman,* Fraser observes that of "these three poets,"
Hendry, Moore, and Treece, "Hendry is the least able to escape into
any private world: he has no dreams, there is nothing about love or
friendship, or even making a living, not one touch of autobiography

in all his verse." Hendry's *The Orchestral Mountain* partly remedies such deficiencies. Hendry has dreams, some of which suggest utopian fulfillment. Personal and social fragmentation is remedied as the poet finds reintegration or wholeness, the Apocalyptic objective, in the sonnet beginning "Come to-day then into a new land":

> Come to-day then into a new land
> Where all made new is wonder whole again.
> Dew and the leaves you feel within the hand
> Are part of you. The mystery is made plain.
> Only the agonized man in the needle's eye
> May take this broken toy of world to re-create, . . .
> This, the creation of the sun,
> God's miracle, that never shall be done.[39]

Helmstadter finds that the last two lines of the poem imply "that God's miracle of giving grace to the world will go on forever and never be done or completed. But there is an ambiguity in the line which would permit it to be read that God's miracle would never be done or accomplished."[40] The ambiguity is partly a product of Hendry's echoing Christ's prayer for the establishment of the Kingdom which St. John's Apocalypse celebrates: "Thy kingdom come. Thy will be done. . . ."

The elegy contains as well other biblical allusions, all of which have to do with the establishment of God's Kingdom. Hendry's opening "Come to-day then into a new land" alludes to the Old Testament Promised Land, which itself anticipates for Christians Christ's Messianic Kingdom of God: keep My commandments, God tells Moses, "when ye come into the land which I give you. . . ."[41]

Hendry's "all made new is wonder whole again" similarly reflects St. John's vision of a "new heaven and a new earth . . . Behold, I make all things new."[42] The image of the "agonized man in the needle's eye" echoes Christ's eschatological references to the Kingdom: ". . . it is easier for a camel to go through a needle's eye, than for a rich man to enter the kingdom of God."[43]

As in Lawrence's "A New Heaven and a New Earth" and Thomas's "Author's Prologue," apocalyptic imagery in Hendry's poem becomes a projection of an internal metamorphosis or rebirth. It will "Never" be "done" because it is Romantic process rather than product, personal growth toward wholeness, self-realization, and individuation rather than cosmic event. Rather than beginning in the future, the process, as the opening line suggests, may begin "to-day." As in Maslow's concept of self-actualization, it involves regaining a sense of wonder or awe, freshness of experience, and a sense of fusion with the environment that overcomes subject-object distinctions and the prison-house of subjectivity: "Dew and the leaves you feel within the hand/Are part of you." It is a personal apocalypse or revelation: "The mystery is made plain."

   Other Poems.   More explictly about war than *The Orchestral Mountain* is Hendry's "Midnight Air-Raid," which describes London's civilians as "Freedom's involuntary fighters," stumbling from the "underworld of dreams" to the flickering black and white underworld of bomb shelters:

> Now sirens unleash civilian anguish. In a reflex they
> Stumble from an underworld of dreams whom abortive desire,
> Pillared in moonlit limbs, makes gray;
> Freedom's involuntary fighters, knowing no refuge save
>   in fiery
> Consciousness, rampant light and the resolution of day.
>
> . . . .
>
> Here artist and scientist concur to admire
> A formal pattern of battle, where herring-bone squadrons
> Elude the swaying bars of light, and white fire,
> From London's living furnace, flung up like a tilted
>   cauldron. . . .[44]

In Day-Lewis's "Bombers" the aircraft carry "harm in/Their wombs," an "iron embryo" delivered in "screeching fire." Treece's image of "the bomber's egg" in *Towards a Personal Armageddon* (Part XIII) works similarly to fuse and confuse in Gothic combinations life and death, the organic and the mechanic, and innocence and culpability, and to communicate an attitude of fearful expectancy. In "Midnight Air-Raid," Hendry also finds impending birth symbolic of impending doom. What is delivered is "Anaerobic death," that is, death through smoke and suffocation:

> Sensitive fingers of searchlights pick the pockets of day
> They are surgeon's pitiless forceps imprisoning in their
> grip
> Anaerobic death, there, in the heart of air, lurking
> To burst the harmless tissues of cities.

Hendry's imagery simultaneously suggests impending doom as "Anaerobic death" "lurking" like a beast ready to pounce on its innocuous prey. (More generally reacting to the threat of total war, George Woodcock, like "uncertain and afraid" Auden in "September 1, 1939," writes in "Poem for September, 1939": "The violence we loathe/Crouches above us like an iron beast/Searing our future with a phosgene breath.")

Sound imagery complements visual imagery in such apocalyptic art: judgment-day trumpets (cf. Revelation 8:6ff. and Shelley's "Clarion" in "Ode to the West Wind")—Gabriel to "blow my bone loud" in Barker's "Holy Poems" and "Blowing bone to trumpet stick" in Hendry's "Apocalypse"; thunder, borrowing from St. John's "seven thunders" in Revelation, or doomsday thunder transmuted into the thunderous sounds of artillery—the "lightning" "While blinded shell and body's thunder churn" in Hendry's "Golgotha"; droning enemy bombers; and air-raid sirens—Spender's "Cassandra bell" in "Epilogue to a Human Drama" and Hendry's "sirens" which "unleash civilian anguish" in "Midnight Air-Raid."

The anticipated German invasion of England in 1940—code named by the Germans *Seelöwe* ("Sea Lion")—contributes to the atmosphere of impending doom in Neo-Romantic art, as in Comfort's ambiguous "Waiting for the Wind" and Hendry's "London Before Invasion," in which bombed

> Walls and buildings stand here still, like shells.
> Hold them to the ear. There are no echoes even
> Of the seas that once were.
>
> . . . .
>
> Flood-tides returning may bring with them blood and fire.
> Blenching with wet panic spirit that must be rock.
> May bring a future tossed and torn, as slippery as wrack.
> All time adrift in torrents of blind war.

Nineteenth-century Romantics also anticipated invasion, as in Wordsworth's 1803 "Lines On the Expected Invasion" by the French. But Romantic poetry is less fearful and terrifying, partly because of the absence of the imminent threat of fire-bombing and Spender's depressing conclusion that a world in war may in effect achieve, if not the end of the world, the end of civilization.

In "The Reflex of History," Hendry, like Read and Aldous Huxley, finds Pavlovian reflex (stimulus-response) conditioning suitable to explain the behavior of the dehumanized, mechanized, and visionless soldier and citizen of authoritarian societies: "Marching these men know without knowledge, see without vision." Like Treece, Hendry sometimes presents the artist, in contrast to such visionless conformists, as a prophet, often unheeded by an insensitive public, who is able to see with Wordsworth "into the life of things" and become an interpreter. In "The Death of Milton,"[45] Hendry depicts Milton as beset, like Lear, with insensitive daughters. What they miss (a prophet hath honor, "save in his own country, and in his own house,"[46]) is sightless Milton's fabulous role as a seer:

> In darkness see the moon, singled out, and slow snow scour
> Detached and still, the sealed eyes of this seer
> Whole tempest, shaking the ocean's hoar flower
> Bring all our dead to birth in the white grief of Lear.

Appropriately a sonnet for sonnet-making Milton, the poem continues by paying homage as well to the libertarian Milton of *Areopagitica*. Milton's humanitarian art rises above domestic discord and above St. Paul's Cathedral oppressed by the Blitz:

> Their bright teeth through his winter mock like rime,
> Flashing swords in the immortal theatre of a poetry
> That crumbles towers of hours of tyranny and crime.

> St. Paul's, crowned by searchlights and haloed by doom,
> Still rearing high its mind, is not so high
> As this old man in his abandoned room
> Of blindness rising up in light to die.

> Blow, horns of silence. An overburdened head rests
>   upon air.
> And, sun of grief, strew your bright diamonds on his hair.

"Ode On a Chinese Scroll" is an ecumenical vision of a world united in a common bond of suffering. Finding in such awareness of oneness an antidote to social disintegration, as well as all we know on earth and all we need to know (Keats's "truth and beauty"), Hendry adapts the biblical metaphor of "tongues of fire" which allowed Christ's disciples in Acts to communicate universally by being given the supernatural gift of tongues:

> Our truth and beauty
> Speak with the tongues of flags. Shall they be furled?
> Shall brutality and lie bring them dumb
> To the scaffold of the centuries
> O nation whose tears are the rivers of the world?

Hendry's "tongues of flags" recall Spender's "tongues of flame" image in "Rejoice in the Abyss," another poem about fellow suffering and compassion in war.

In "Adonai," Hendry fuses Christ, out of whose spear-pierced side came blood and water, and, implied by the title, Adonis, who is similarly resurrected in the spring from Hell and from whose wounds came the flower, anemone. Hendry's Adonis-Christ thus becomes a variation of the archetypal hero whose death paradoxically produces life. In stanza three, Moses and Elijah, "Felled by the blood of unbelieving day," undergo an analogous spiritual resurrection, as "the stars/Of Heaven in their pride/Burst through the trees of Hell. . . ." The poem's title is from the Hebrew *Adonai,* the Jewish substitution for the ineffable name of their Diety, Yahweh, and suggests the ineffable mystery and sanctity of such processes in the realm of the spirit:

> How if blood and water
> In his body come together
> Dissolution shall ensue.
> There shall be no issue.
> Flesh shall be a gushet

Wherein blood and waterfall,
Blades of parting shears,
May wither into Lethe. . . .

How Moses and Elijah lay
Dead in Jerusalem's streets,
Felled by the blood of unbelieving day, . . .
Twin sons of thunder, when the stars
Of Heaven in their pride
Burst through the trees of Hell. . . .

How, out of secret Samothrace
Stole the jealous Kabiri, guards
Against all ecstasy, who curdle
Milk and chill the youthful veins,
Inviolate in their union;
Switching fertile water's aspiration
Into Blood's assassinate ambition. . . .

Hendry similarly fuses Moses and Elijah, his "Twin sons of thunder,"
with his Kabiri, "who curdle/Milk." The imagery seems drawn
partly from Lawrence's *Apocalypse*. Lawrence notes that the Kabiri are
"twins" and are called " 'sons of thunder.' " According to Lawrence,
they have the ability "to curdle milk" and "turn water into blood."[47]
   Hendry's "Adonai" is also another Romantic poem about reconciling divergent forms of awareness. Lawrence writes that if "the water
and blood ever mingled in our bodies, we should be dead," adding
that the "two streams are kept apart" by the twin Kabiri: "And on
the two streams depends the dual consciousness": our "day-concious-
ness and our night-consciousness. . . ."[48] In addition, Hendry's
"There shall be no issue,/Flesh shall be a gushet" creates further paradox through its phallic, orgasmic suggestiveness. Lawrence sees the
Kabiri as "the secret lords of sex" and, perhaps providing the stimulus for Hendry's associational thinking, writes that they also are "the
two candlesticks which stand before the lord of earth, Adonai."[49]

Chapter Three
Henry Treece

Introduction

Henry Treece is a prolific writer. His poetry is largely contained in seven volumes. His literary criticism includes *Dylan Thomas: "Dog Among the Fairies"* (1949), the first book on Thomas, and *How I See Apocalypse* (1946). He is also the author of a play (1955), a collection of short stories (1946), and, between 1952 and 1968, thirty-six novels and six "thrillers for children." Treece has also written histories (*Three Crusades,* 1962, as well as four histories for children); editions (*Herbert Read: An Introduction to His Work by Various Hands,* 1944, and *A Selection of Poems from Swinburne,* 1948); and twelve anthologies, eight coedited with Stefan Schimanski and three Apocalyptic anthologies with J. F. Hendry.

"I was born just before the Great War of 1914–18 and grew to school-age with a fear of *The Germans* greater than that of witches, ghosts, or vampire-bats," Treece begins his *How I See Apocalypse.*[1] When war again broke out, Treece joined the Royal Air Force. ". . . I am Welsh and have little love for the English, so it's not 'patriotism' that drives me," Treece explains in a 15 September 1941 letter to Comfort, adding, "But there, I am talking nonsense; the fact is that I do not think about it—I only feel that I have to go."[2] To pacifist anarchists, such as Tolstoy, Woodcock, or Comfort, Treece's commitment to the war effort would have seemed unacceptable. But militant models for Treece were available in Kropotkin's support of the Allies against Germany in the First World War and Read's support of England's efforts in the Second World War.

Critical opinion of Henry Treece's poetry has differed sharply. Although Treece was an "excessive admirer of Dylan Thomas," the "admiration wasn't mutual," Nicholas Moore recalls.[3] T. S. Eliot, however, said to Treece that he "impressed him more than any poet for

twenty years," Treece records in a letter dated 18 May 1943 to Denton Welch. Treece adds, "These things make up for the spite of the
Little People."[4]

Treece's unpopularity is partly the consequence of his sometimes
taking Thomas's principle of condensation to excess. Writing to
Treece, Thomas explains that " 'much' " of the " 'obscurity' " of his
poetry " 'is due to rigorous compression.' " Thomas's defense of his
poetry is in response to Stephen Spender's criticism: " 'The truth is
that Thomas's poetry is turned on like a tap; it is just poetic stuff
with no beginning nor end, or intelligent and intelligible control.' "[5]

Much of Treece's condensed imagery is in Freudian language imagery which is "over-determined," or may be interpreted in several
ways simultaneously. Essentially rational or logical linkage of words
and images, more characteristic of the poetry of the Auden group,
gives way to associational linkages of both images and words: puns,
assonance, alliteration, and metaphysical conceits joining things apparently unlike.

Treece's imagery is also confusing inasmuch as there is in Treece's
poetry, as well as Neo-Romantic poetry generally, less of a clear
boundary between inner and outer experiences.

Neo-Romantic poets such as Treece, moreover, are both simpler
and more complex than the poets that preceded them. They are simpler in the way that Wordsworth and Coleridge are simpler than
Pope and Dryden by way of being less topically allusive. They are
simpler than Eliot and Pound in being less literately allusive. But
allusions, where they appear, are more likely to be private and,
hence, potentially undecipherable.

Neo-Romantic art, furthermore, is more primitive and childlike
than the art of Pound, Eliot, Auden, and earlier writers inasmuch as
it sometimes represents a more regressive, archaic, less conceptually
sophisticated level of mental functioning. But it is sometimes more
complex in its syntactical and symbolical density. As in Imagism,
concentration is valued in the poetry of Treece, Barker, Hendry,
Comfort, and Thomas. But the concentration is of the multiple
meanings attached to symbols or clusters of symbols. A two-dimen-
sional diagram of a Neo-Romantic poem would often not be a
straight line, as in logical or chronological or narrative development,
but an oscillating progression, like an electroencephalogram.

Poems of *The New Apocalypse*

Treece includes one of his short stories, "The Brindled Cow," in the first Apocalyptic anthology, *The New Apocalypse*. Surrealistic metamorphosis of the secure daylight world of consciousness and predictability dissolving into its opposite is Treece's subject. Kafka's influence is apparent in Treece's description of the transformation of the brindled cow which Jane leads: "Aaiie! moaned the cow, and, behold! where she had stood was now a phosphorescent lobster." It is partly symbolic of Jane's or Treece's sense of depersonalization in an unstable environment. The nightmare is that of modern technological, mass society which erodes the individual's reassuring relationship with the natural environment and impersonalizes and objectifies human experience:

At sundown Jane led the brindled cow over the hill. . . . As they passed between the hedges, honey-suckle called out to them in a soft sweet voice. . . . A circling peewit . . . called down. And a mouse in the furze at the edge of the wood called across.

Only Jane noticed these invitations. . . .

But suddenly the black cloud above the spire opened its mouth, and from between its cankered yellow teeth shot row upon row of dazzling lightnings. Thunder rolled with a Miltonic clatter . . . Brouhaha! Brouhauhaha! Jane smelt the singed hide, and heard the hot blood gushing into the ditch. . . . A black cat burst through the hedge and shot screaming through the furze that carpeted the wood. . . .

Jane, by this time, felt no doubt that she was becoming a copy of the cheaper Daily Press. . . .

Her mind grew more contented, and fainter. . . . Her hands grew into a Comic Strip, and her feet into a Sports Page, and her eyes into the Society Column. . . . And she blanched, and bent double, and fell flat in the dust.

Treece's references to an ominous "black cloud," "dazzling lightnings," and thunder rolling with "Miltonic clatter" suggest that Jane is confronted by a miniaturized apocalypse. The pattern of the story itself suggests the implications of apocalyptic visions generally in the late 1930s and 1940s.

Visions of the catastrophic end of world history may function as projections, sometimes unconscious, of repressed anxieties concerning personal annihilation or death. The poet's terror of personal disinte-

gration is expressed or projected in awesome apocalyptic imagery of
a disintegrating cosmos. The way toward such indirect symbolic
expression of death anxiety seems already prepared by Thomas, who,
in "Especially When the October Wind" (1934), concludes,

> The heart is drained that, spelling in the scurry
> Of chemic blood, warned of the coming fury.
> By the sea's side hear the dark-vowelled birds.

The "coming fury," according to William York Tindall, "is a Miltonic confusion of the third fate (Atropos and her 'abhorred shears')
with the third fury, Megaera."[6] But the "coming fury," as in Mac-
beth's "sound and fury,/Signifying nothing," suggests, more directly, outbursts of rage and turbulence: in context, the winter turbulence which the cold October wind anticipates or helps to create.
Perhaps alluding to the gathering stormclouds in Europe in the
1930s, Thomas uses impending outward disaster in Nature and European civilization to express indirectly his continuing preoccupation
with impending death.

The relationship between Apocalypticism and Neo-Romanticism
generally and Surrealism may also be reinterpreted in such a context.
Read, who acquiesced peacefully in the contemplation of death as a
natural process, by popularizing Surrealism as an aesthetic technique
for exploring the unconscious, contributed to the full-blown incorporation into English poetry of a Surrealist technique through which
Romantic death consciousness in general, and the insecurity of the
war years in particular, may be consciously or unconsciously expressed. As in the paintings of Dominguez, Dali, Oelze, and Magritte, or as in Heidegger, the environment and the self in much
Neo-Romantic poetry are on the brink of disintegrating or dissolving
or slipping away into nothingness.

The normal categories of experience and the predictable world,
moreover, are replaced by puzzling ambiguity and unpredictability.
By contrast, Read rejected specifically the Existentialist view, also at
work implicitly in Neo-Romanticism generally, of "the terrifying nature of our human predicament," which leaves the frail, finite individual in *"Angst."*[7]

The most apocalyptic-sounding of Treece's poems appearing in *The*

New Apocalypse is his ten-stanza *Towards a Personal Armageddon—for J. F. Hendry.* In a 15 September 1941 letter to Comfort, Treece proudly notes that "Eliot calls it [the poem] 'distinguished'."

Treece describes *Towards a Personal Armageddon* as an "elaborate and highly textured metaphysical" poem, "full of conceits and personal references."[8] Its sonnet-sequence structure and opening image of the "shapes of Truth" may be indebted to Thomas's *Altarwise by Owl-Light*:

> The shapes of Truth are no man's history
> Or hope; born in the horny womb of Time,
> They die with the daylight, ere the Surgeon's hand
> Can grasp the knife to solve the mystery
> Of feeling and the half-formed word. Sand
> Trickles slily through the palm like this,
> Playing the hour-glass with the living bone,
> Wife to the midnight sigh, the foetal wish.

Treece's Surrealistic image of the "sand" that plays "hour-glass" and "wife to the midnight sigh" is reminiscent of Breton's image of *le sable* ("sand") that is but a *horloge* ("clock") which says *minuit* ("midnight") through the arms of a woman in "Tout Paradis n'est pas Perdu." It is also another Thomasesque *memento mori* image linking sexuality, procreation, and death.

Partly in order to negate stereotyped modes of perception and increase the associative richness of his poetry, Thomas fragments language and image. For example, in "If I Were Tickled by the Rub of Love," *lockjaw* is the implied pun in Thomas's images of "the lock/Of sick old manhood on the fallen jaws. . . ." Barker's implied *road gang* in "Elegy V" works similarly: "Hosannas on the tongues of the dumb shall raise/Roads for the gangs in chains to return to/God." The context of Treece's poem allows "surgeon" to be interpreted as delivering pediatrician, or midwife, whose knife cuts the baby's umbilical cord, and *midwife* is suggested by his images of sand or bone as "Wife to the midnight sigh."

Such language distortions reflect a sense of inner and outer disintegration, as well as a revival of the Romantic imagination which, like sleep, "dissolves, diffuses, dissipates," in Coleridge's language, "in order to recreate." In the second half of stanza one, Treece describes the poet:

> The tired poet in his reeling room
> Twists thoughts to clothe his bare hypnotic words;
> Distracted by the rain on sodden thatch,
> He moves towards the window, lifts the latch,
> Cries, crazed by some bloody incubus of doom,
> "Oh, listen to the laughter of the birds!"

The image of the poet-prophet as mentally deranged or half-crazed appears elsewhere in apocalyptic visionary literature, as in Wordsworth's apocalyptic dream vision in *The Prelude* of a "semi-Quixote," "crazed" Arab prophet,[9] and Barker's "Vision of England '38" in which Blake appears as a lamb, announcing, "I am Blake who broke my mind on God." In Coleridge's "Kubla Khan," a possible model having apocalyptic elements, the visionary experience is similarly maddening and hypnotic.

More generally, the device of a demented persona, influenced partly by Romanticism and Surrealism, is revived in Treece's poetry and fiction and in other Neo-Romantic works, such as Derek Stanford's "The Orchard and the Sin," a poem which similarly relies on nineteenth-century models: Stanford presents his narrator as another Coleridgean or Byronic guilt-ridden, exiled, eternal wanderer, with supporting features, such as the journey motif, "the void," the "moor," and "the magic wood," also indebted partly to his Romantic precursors.

Attempting again art which is multidimensional, Treece in *Selections from a Poem in Progress* treats modern death consciousness in language probably influenced by Eliot's *The Waste Land* (". . . Those are pearls that were his eyes."):

> Now Time has painted dearth across my heart
> And those are corals that were once my eyes
> I sit, watching the winter's breath upon
> The pane. Under a cloven cloak a man
> Offers his twitching twigs for my poor crumbs.
> Is it my father? Beneath his rag a bone
> Box grins riddles from its wormy holes.

"Cloven cloak" and "bone box" symbolize, among other things, female genitalia. "Bone" by itself (cf. Thomas's "winged bone" or Miller's "bone" in Chapter 1 of *Tropic of Cancer*) and "stone swinging on hempen cords" are phallic. But what drops from father is not simply seed or semen (cf. Thomas's "Shall it be male or female? say the cells,/And drop the plum like fire from the flesh."), but Kafkaesque reminders of the poet's mortality or creatureliness:

> I see a stone swinging on hempen cords
> Between his cage's bars where no bird sings;
> My loaf he takes, he takes my love of life
> Under his creeping tatters forked to his side;
> I shudder as I watch my father's hairs
> Drop rats and scorpions, shudder as I find
> My flesh-bare fingers folding over ants!

More Oedipally obsessed than Thomas, Treece implies a potentially castrating father ("Time" becomes Father), whose sex organ, an intimidating dominance signal from an ethological perspective, or swinging scythe means impotency or death. The barred cage, the equivalent of "the cage of sex" in Barker's "Secular Elegy V," is clearly in father's rather than Oedipally desirous son's possession.

The image of the "stone swinging on hempen cords" in the final stanza is metamorphosed into the Oedipally awesome, coffinlike, "six-foot cedar swinging through the ground." "Dry sticks," in the line "From the dry sticks no gushing oil can leap," continues to have the impotency, Oedipally intimating meanings of the earlier image of "twitching twigs," with "gushing oil" having the orgasmic associations of Thomas's "Light Breaks Where No Sun Shines" in which the "gushers of the sky" divine the "oil of tears." Olson notes that Thomas "uses an odd form of periphrasis which makes a familiar thing unfamiliar by describing it accurately but in the manner of a primitive definition: thus, 'shafted disk' for 'clock,' 'bow-and-arrow birds' for 'weathercocks.' "[10] Treece's "bone box" represents a similar paraphrase in primitive diction. In addition to its sexual implications, it represents the coffin as a box for human bones, as the poem's last stanza indicates: ". . . from his box no word may wind. . . ."

In Neo-Romantic poetry, the wind, which turns the weather vane around, is sometimes symbolic of unusually unpleasant developments, such as the onset of aging and undesirable changes in social status. It is in this sense the modern equivalent of the medieval wheel of fortune. For example, Treece in the "Poem" beginning "After a little while" uses the wind as an ambivalent symbol of unpleasant developments, freedom, and youthful vitality. He remembers himself as a child

> . . . whose needs
> Were those alone that motivate the birds
> To ride wild winds or rest content in woods.
> But after faith and fame the gale blew round,
> Back to its caverned home, and left him loose.

Treece's imagery is similar to Thomas's in "Poem in October" in which Treece's "gale" is "wind" and "blew round" is "turned around": "There could I marvel/My birthday/Away," Thomas exclaims, "but the weather turned around."

"Speech for Hamlet" appears to reflect Ernest Jones's well-known psychoanalytic approach to Hamlet. The center of Hamlet's Oedipal lust, Gertrude, is also a Circe figure in Treece's poem. Like Shakespeare's irresolute hero, Treece's Hamlet in facing death finds, in Shakespeare's language, that his "native hue of resolution/Is sicklied o'er with the pale cast of thought":

> The Queen, man's mistress, mastered me in wrongs,
> Then plucked my eyes to feed her noble swine. . . .
> Heart-high the callow hangman swings my fears,
> My scarecrow deeds that shudder in the night. . . .

Eliotesque sex nausea is also included to heighten the ambivalence of Hamlet's Oedipal conflict. At birth and during sexual intercourse, in fantasy rather than fact, presumably, Hamlet is between the lips of the vulva and its pubic hairs. The image of the "female sticks" is borrowed from Thomas's "If I Were Tickled by the Rub of Love" in which the poet "Broke through the straws," mindful of the "crossed sticks of war." Treece's imagery suggests among other things the sorts of sexual activity which contradict cultural conditioning and would normally be shot through with guilt or anxiety about impending punishment or "hell": cunnilingus and Oedipally incestuous union within a context of Thomasesque death consciousness which relentlessly permeates sexual activity or desire:

> Between the female sticks I tasted hell
> Garnished with flowers. Under its mask the skull
> Mocked my poor flesh's labour, foisted the lilt
> Of lust upon me, led me a dance and laughed
> At body's fever. Dour death in bone
> Bent my frail twig, turned song to stone.

The fact that incest is universally horrifying, making the incest taboo the only universal moral prohibition, may have motivated Treece and Hendry's selection of Thomas's "The Burning Baby" for *The New Apocalypse*. Thomas's story is made even more horrifying because the child produced by the incestuous union of the father, Rhys Rhys, a vicar, and his daughter, is cremated:

It was, they said, on a fine sabbath morning in the middle of summer that Rhys Rhys fell in love with his daughter. . . . He told her that she was more beautiful than her dead mother. . . . The folds of her dress could not hide from him the shabby nakedness of her body. . . .

Rhys Rhys, over the bouldered rim, led her to terror. He sighed and sprang at her. She mixed with him in the fourth and fifth terrors of the flesh. . . .

And the baby caught fire. The flames curled round its mouth and blew upon the shrinking gums. Flame round its red cord lapped its little belly till the raw flesh fell upon the heather. A flame touched its tongue. Eeech, cried the burning baby, and the illuminated him replied.[11]

In this respect, the art of both Treece and Thomas is Gothic, for Gothicism, from Walpole's *The Mysterious Mother* to Murdoch's *A Severed Head,* exploits incest for terrifying effects. That other types of socially unacceptable sexual behavior may function almost as well to invoke a Gothic, Kafkaesque atmosphere, is Dorian Cook's premise in "Ray Scarpe: Part I: The Man from the Vision of Nothing," also in *The New Apocalypse*:

He grew: and the years of his life became the spine of a terrible army in
battle, more barren than all the Easter females who touched his body and
tore him with their metal frames: year of the rotting monster, years to be
consumed between the legs of electric sluts, forked-lightning shadows of a
dream scuffle. . . . In the Juggernaut city he saw the drunken children of
harlots crushed under the wheels. . . . 'Ray Scarpe!' shrieked the women of
the eaten-away slum; they sucked his name into their thin paunches where
it coiled among iron entrails and bruised itself on fleshless liquids.[12]

The emphasis on terror in Apocalyptic and Neo-Romantic art has
other causes. It echoes the nightmarish atmosphere of horror and violence in Surrealism. Treece's emphasis on terror, moreover, reflects
that of earlier apocalyptic works, such as the prophetic poems of Shelley and Blake, as well as Wordsworth's apocalyptic vision in *The Prelude,* which causes him to wake "in terror."[13] Barker in his apocalyptic
"Elegy No. I" depicts an air-born apocalyptic beast, or latter-day
pterodactyl, which covers with "horror the green Abyssinian meadow,"
while intimidating, as does *Apocalypse Now,* that the terrifying beast
of the apocalypse does not simply descend in flight from the heavens
but ascends as well from the murky regions of the Id. In addition,
the Neo-Romantic linking of terror and art, or assumption that terror
in poetry engenders the experience of the beautiful or sublime, has
behind it the speculations of Poe, Burke, Baudelaire, and Rilke, as
in his "Die Erste Elegie" argument *das Schöne* or "beauty" is *nichts/als
des Schrecklichen Anfang, den wir noch grade ertragen,* nothing but the
commencement of terror, or the dreadful, that we are still able to
endure.

The emphasis on terror and violence in the art of Treece, Thomas,
Cooke, Gascoyne, Patchen, and Hendry is also in response to the terrifying objective conditions of world history in the late 1930s and
1940s. Both Neo-Romanticism and Existentialism in effect take the
Gothic tradition, in which a sense of impending doom is a conventional ingredient, and breathe new life into it by demonstrating its
modern psychological and sociological relevance. Conventional gothic
dread of the undead becomes Existential and Neo-Romantic dread of
impending doom or nothingness, which may have been at the basis
of Gothicism all along.

Poems of the Prince

Surveying the achievements of the Apocalyptic Movement, Walford Morgan writes, "It is well to note here the remarkable achievements which characterize this phase [i.e., before Personalism]—particularly Henry Treece's *Ballad of the Prince,* and J. F. Hendry's *The Orchestral Mountain,* both of which in power of sustained imagery and rich lyrical vision bear comparison with any verse written in the last decade."[14] Derek Stanford similarly argues that Treece's ballad is "one of the most successful long poems since the war."[15] Comfort in *Poetry Quarterly* praises Treece's ballad as "the fullest expression of the ideals of the [Apocalyptic] school"; "its frank romanticism and lyrical imagery stand in the tradition of legend, and for the form Treece has returned to Spenser."[16]

An interest in medieval art in general and ballads in particular characterizes as well late-eighteenth- and nineteenth-century Romanticism, to which Treece also seems indebted. Rather than choosing "low and rustic life" after the manner of Wordsworth, however, Treece presents Christ as a variation of the conventional gallant knight of medieval ballads, who is the predictable object of revenge and love: in Treece's poem, Satan's revenge and Mary's love.

In *The Ballad of the Prince* Treece also revives the technique of alliterative compound adjectives of earlier ballads and Anglo-Saxon poetry, as in his *Beowulf*-like reference to "halls" in which "wine-heated harp should twang."[17] He revives in his poetry generally the technique of Anglo-Saxon kennings. For example, the "green shark-cradles" in his "The Dyke Builder" means *waves* and is reminiscent of the Anglo-Saxon kenning "whale-road" for *ocean.* Sometimes Treece heightens the Anglo-Saxon atmosphere of such kennings through alliteration, as in his "Woe-worker, Herod's henchman" in "Poem for Christmas." Barker's compounds are probably influencial in this repect, as in Barker's "woe-womb of the want-raped mind" in "Epistle I." Sometimes Treece's alliterative compounds increase the verbal complexity of the poems in which they appear. For example, in Treece's "Remembering Last Year," a rearrangement of words from the biblical crucifixion descriptions—the thorns on Christ's head and the spear piercing his side or breast—allows a compound word, "spearhead," which already exists in the language, to have multiple meanings, while qualifying the meaning of "thorn"; "the small thorn like spearhead in my breast."

The view of Christ presented in *The Ballad of the Prince* is of course heterodox. But there are antecedents, such as Pound's "Ballad of the Goodly Fere," which emphasizes or discovers Christ's manliness, and "The Dream of the Rood," in which Christ is similarly presented as a young warrior.

Like Thomas and Comfort, Treece moves from complexity toward simplicity. For example, "The Second Coming," which reworks the Christian view of the apocalypse, has little of the syntactical density and congestion of imagery of his earlier poems. But the poem does retain a Surrealistic confusion of time and fusion of symbolic roles: Christ is again presented as a warrior-prince.

Treece's "Sermon in the Field" (Part IV) borrows from Christ's sermon on the mount.[18] Christ is presented as an archetypal hero, involved in a cycle of death and renewal, as well as a combination of prince, warrior, and poet or bard. In "Resurrection" (Part I), Treece's image of "the young nun" and image of the ghostly Christ as a "tortured spirit" crossing a seemingly English "heath" have a nineteenth-century Gothic and Surrealistic effect. Similar dreamlike distortions and condensations of time and place are involved in "Sermon in the Field." The Bethlehem oxen low as St. Peter's cock crows, telescoping Christ's birth and death, in somewhat the manner that Treece and Thomas telescope their own in their secular poetry:

> The Prince walked out in purple,
> He galloped out in gold
> To speak with all the people
> That stood in Judas' field.
>
> His black hair hung in ringlets
> All bound with silver bands,
> And gay hawks shod with opals
> Stood on his jewelled hands.
>
> The people heard his gospels, . . .
>
> Until a child's voice shattered
> The magic by a word,

"Look! Underneath his golden coat
There's blood upon his side!"

And as the words were spoken
A cock began to crow,
And from the village stables
We heard the oxen low.

They tore off all the purple,
They quarrelled for his gold,
And left the gay hawks broken
And dying in the field.

"To the Edge and Back"

"To the Edge and Back" appears in *The Black Seasons* (1945) and is
as well the only poem by Treece included in the last Apocalyptic anthology, *The Crown and the Sickle*. The poem shows "Treece becoming
less Apocalyptic," Helmstadter argues.[19] Like Voltaire's Candide,
Treece at the poem's conclusion learns, in effect, to tend his garden:

I have been where none have [*sic*] been before;
I have seen what none should ever see;
And now the calf is crying to be fed.

I do not want to go there any more,
For if I go I fear that I shall stay.
Who would remember then to wind the clock?

Treece's medievalism and exoticism recall John Bayliss's poetry which
less religiously revives a strain of Romanticism going back to Keats,
Poe, and the more exotic, supernatural, and sensuous works of Coleridge, Shelley, and Byron: Bayliss's "Legend," for example, treats
medieval castles, magic, and the supernatural, evil (or sadism) in conflict with good, and frustrating, unsatisfiable desire; while his "The
Lost Princess" revives Romantic fascination with lost ladies, pedestalized women, and obsessional, self-destructive, seemingly masochistic
romantic love. Both Treece and Bayliss may have developed away
from such exoticism partly because it is not likely to be accepted by
most modern readers. Jean Cocteau had recommended a more viable

technique in *Le Secret Professionnel* in arguing that poets avoid exotic or strange topics in attempts to startle their readers. The function of poetry, by contrast, is to disclose or reveal the common things around us which habit has kept us from appreciating in all their pristine, remarkable splendor, or so Cocteau believed. In this sense, the poem implies Treece's departure from the baroque fantasizing and Apocalyptic visions of his earlier poetry, and the poem may be viewed as a hybrid which incorporates, among other things, a variation of the Romantic vision-is-fled theme of Coleridge, Keats, and Wordsworth.

But it would be an overstatement to conclude that the poem shows Treece philosophically becoming less Apocalyptic. In a 16 January 1944 letter to Hendry (written in the same year that *The Crown and the Sickle* was published), Treece reaffirms his commitment to Apocalyptic principles. Referring to a review which implied that Treece had seceded from the Apocalyptic movement, Treece writes to Hendry,

I would like you to write an answer, and let me join you in signing the letter. We can sign as a pair of writers, and our solid front will give the lie to the reviewer.

I wish to state here categorically that I have not seceded from Apoc. If Staples could have found paper earlier all the world would have seen that we are still working together. The Crown and S. shd. settle that doubt. . . .

I am too proud of my associations with Apoc. to scuttle it; and the reviewer shows a most lamentable lack of knowledge of me to suggest it. I was annoyed, and thought to write to him personally, but was unable to do so owing to work.

In politics, I can only see Anarchism as a future; though I shd. be at variance very often with Woodcock's version.

Anyway, I support you in anything you care to say to the Tribune. I have faith in you, and in our association.[20]

Other critical perspectives warrant reexamination. According to Baggerly, "To the Edge and Back" is a "long poem" in which Treece "presents the 'black seasons' of madness, the vision of an insane man in which the despair of all history is seen."[21] Describing the poem's narrative structure, Helmstadter writes that "It tells how a poet falls asleep and dreams he goes back through Time to the beginning of Time itself; he goes right to the edge of Nothing. Confronted with sheer nothingness, man desires to make a myth explaining the vacuum. The poet in the dream, however, makes a silly myth, a pun on the 'In the beginning was the word.' "[22]

Part Three of "To the Edge and Back," which begins "In the beginning was the bird," Treece anthologizes in his *Air Force Poetry* (1944), and Comfort and Bayliss include in their *New Road 1943*. Similarly, Oscar Williams selected the Part-Three poem for his anthology *A Pocket Book of Modern Verse* (1954). Myth-making is involved, as in a punning allusion to the New-Testament fusion of Hebrew (Genesis 1:1) and Greek (*logos* philosophizing) myths about the origin of the world. (Cf. *How I See Apocalypse* in which Treece refers to a "revolt" that "takes the shape of a counter-myth . . . .")[23] The bird is "God's defence," evidence of some element of purposeful activity in the biological and physical evolution of the universe. It may be "Before man" in part because it is, like Lawrence's similarly reptilian symbol in "Tortoise Gallantry," man's "Fore-runner" (in Lawrence's language) in evolution. (Cf. also Lawrence's "Humming-Bird," which playfully considers the humming-bird's more reptilian ancestry "Before anything had a soul. . . .") All of Part III of Treece's poem reads:

> In the beginning was the bird
> A spume of feathers on the face of time,
> Man's model for destruction, God's defence.
>
> Before man, a bird, a feather before time,
> And music growing outward into space,
> The feathered shears cutting dreams in air.
>
> Before birds, a God, a Nothing with a shape
> More horrible than mountains or the Plague
> A voice as large as fate, a tongue of bronze.
>
> Before this, O no before was there.
> Where? Among the placeless atoms, mad
> As tale the maggot makes locked in the skull.
>
> And so I state a bird. For sanity
> My brain's lips blow the tumbled plume.
> I see it prophesy the path the winds take.

Earlier critics bypass the literary tradition in which Treece is writing. "To the Edge and Back" is first of all a dream vision. Its opening stanza implies its dream-vision format:

> Sleep comes to Princes in their beds
> And to the shepherd underneath a bush.
>
> Sleep shuts the eyes of the murderous owl
> And gives tomorrow to the trembling wren.

Such imagery probably owes a debt to Chaucer's visionary *Book of the Duchess,* in which the insomniac poet laments that "nature wolde nat suffyse/To noon erthly creature/Nat long tyme to endure/Withoutte slep and be in sorwe." Furthermore, Treece's use of the phrase "I see" in Parts Three and Eight and his reference to "prophecy" in Part Three hint at the poem's more essential structure. "To the Edge and Back" is an apocalyptic dream vision. The poet in such visions assumes the role of, or may encounter, the prophet-seer.

The significance of Treece's bird is partly that he is "Man's model for destruction," that is, the model, in a literal sense, for the airplanes which are agents of destruction in the air war over London and Berlin.[24] But Treece's imagery is also like that of Barker in his apocalyptic "Elegy No. I," in which the "moth," rather than the "bird," foreshadows the "Fokker," the airplane as instrument of destruction in war:

> Thus in the stage of time the minor moth is small
> But prophesies the Fokker with marvellous wings
> Mottled with my sun's gold and your son's blood.

Treece's imagery recalls as well Eliot's in *Little Gidding* (1942), in which "The dove descending breaks the air/With flame of incandescent terror. . . ." Providing a potential model for either Eliot or Treece, Barker in "Holy Poems" also fuses the dove of peace and of Christ's baptism with the airplane's image. More explicitly prophetic and apocalyptic than either Eliot or Treece, Barker announces,

> . . . I feel, cold as a draught on my arm,
> The spiralling universe like a worm

> Coiling for comfort; and in my mind
> The three-winged dove among my dreams
> Moaning for its apocalyptic home.

Typical of such apocalyptic visions is the presence of a ghostly visitant (cf. Eliot's "Dead Master" in *Little Gidding*) or spiritual guide who functions as an agent through whom the revelation (or apocalypse) is communicated. Like Barker feeling the "spiralling universe" "cold as a draught" (above), Treece records the "atoms' swirl" (Part Two) and an "icy draught" in the presence of his ghostly visitant (Part Eight):

> Come, said the shrouded figure, taking my
> hands in his thin bones. An icy draught
> swept round us, through us, against us,
> driving our frozen bodies up the chill
> stone steps to the fire blackened roof.

Barker's "Vision of England '38" in which Barker is visited by "a ghost," apparently Shelley's, who holds "out its hands in pain,/Looking at me with eyes that supplicated fate," and Woodcock's visionary "Waterloo Bridge," in which Woodcock imagines "Blake in a chariot over St. Pauls" and other "spectres," are similar. The pattern of all these poems owes something to St. John's angelic visitors, the prophet-seers of Wordsworth in *The Prelude* and Coleridge in "Kubla Khan," and Shelley's "grim" guide, Rousseau, in "The Triumph of Life."

Also typical is the incorporation of an imperative command to attend to the visionary spectacle. Such a command signals the spiritual visitant's authority and function. In "To the Edge and Back" it is "Come" and "Look yet more closely and report your vision. . . ." (Part Eight). In St. John's vision it is "What thou seest write," in Shelley's poem it is "Dost thou behold," and in Barker's "Vision of England '38" it is "Look closely" and "wait in Patience."

Apocalyptic poems in the late 1930s and 1940s tend toward either one of two polarized types, which St. John's apocalyptic vision and Hendry's *The Orchestral Mountain* unite: visionary bliss or hell, Dante's *Inferno* or his *Paradiso*. Treece's vision in "To the Edge and Back" is negative rather than positive, and in this context his spirit-

ual guide comes to look more like a Dickensian version of Dante's
Virgil as a guide through hell. In any case, blissful vision of the
"promised Paradise" in which the elect sing God's praises on Mount
Zion is metamorphosed into its mirror opposite, turning dream to
nightmare. Treece includes fiery skywriting partly to enhance his vision's already dilated apocalyptic and Blitz-weary atmosphere, as does
Woodcock in his image in "Waterloo Bridge" of the citizens of an
insane decade "Skywriting madness in incandescent letters." Asked
by the "shrouded figure" to "report" his "vision," Treece or his persona announces,

I scratched the words I heard upon the harsh parapet where I stood. . . .
   And as I wrote, the words appeared upon the
sky above my head in signs of fire, in all the
colours of damnation, and attended by a distant
singing, as of the Sad Ones from under the hill
who find that the promised Paradise is one of
stone and the eternal sobbing of the wind across
a sunless moor.
   And this is what I wrote across heaven:
I see the half-born babe, unkindly formed
Screaming to be taken back from life.

. . . .

         I fell across the plains of Tartary,
         The screaming hell of frozen flame and hate,
         Where hooded figures walk in solitude. . . .
         And God there waiting in the shape of goat,
         His dull eyes smiling, and the hanging lip
         Tasting corruption from the midnight breeze. . . .

Like *Towards a Personal Armageddon*, "To the Edge and Back" presents another version of the poet as half-crazed by his vision, as the
passage above suggests. In paranoid schizophrenic fashion, Treece in
his goat image both projects his feelings of self-condemnation and
that which is being condemned: antisocial and dehumanizing instinc-
tual or animal gratification.
   To put the matter differently, therapeutic introspection takes the
form of the archetypal quest or journey inward to confront or "drag

to light," in Thomas's language, the diseased forces of the soul. "To expose a terror is to conquer it," Treece continues to maintain in the last Neo-Romantic anthology, *A New Romantic Anthology* (1949).[25] It is also the Freudian premise for some of Hitchcock's similarly Gothic and psychoanalytic thrillers. A plausible contemporary antecedent is Edward Upward's Marxist *Journey to the Border* (1938) in which his protagonist journeys through hallucinatory visions to the border of insanity and back.

Surrealism's influence is also important in this respect. As if to interpret the title of his poem for us, Treece earlier in *The New Apocalypse* quotes Henri Barranger's argument that Surrealism leads us to " 'the edge of madness' ":

"Surrealism now aims at recreating *a condition which will be in no way inferior to mental derangement*. Its ambition is to lead us to the edge of madness and make us feel what is going on in the magnificently disordered minds of those whom the community shuts up in asylums."[26]

Treece's intention is to refute the Surrealistic assumption that automatic writing, without conscious and "poetic craftsmanship," is sufficient for poetry. Dylan Thomas is "a superior craftsman to, and a truer poet than any of the surrealists," because he is able to "discipline" the material generated by the unconscious.[27] But Neo-Romantics, such as Thomas and Treece, do suggest in their art some of the conditions of madness. The new uses of old words and invention of new compound words and their congested imagery superficially resemble psychotic neologisms and the sort of stimuli flooding which occurs in schizophrenia. Oddly enough, negative apocalyptic fantasy or end-of-the-world thinking is symptomatic of schizophrenia as well as typical of apocalyptic poems in the 1940s. But rather than having been influenced directly by psychotic fantasizing, the apocalyptic poets of the 1940s have as their models not only an earlier tradition of apocalyptic literature, but the distorted and disturbed images of Van Gogh, Munch, and Grosz, the psychotic imagery and paranoid visions of Kafka's fiction, and the fantasies of psychopathological tyrants in the 1930s and 1940s being enacted in history.

Chapter Four

Apocalyptic Associates: MacCaig, Fraser, and Moore

Norman MacCaig

In "The Apocalyptic Element in Modern Poetry" Hendry lists Norman "McCaig" (as MacCaig's name is spelled in the anthologies of the 1940s) among the "members of the original apocalyptic group."[1] Similarly, in *How I See Apocalypse,* Treece affirms that the Apocalyptic Movement "had as its first poetic enthusiasts J. F. Hendry, Nicholas Moore, and Norman McCaig. . . ."[2] MacCaig's early enthusiasm was not about the New Apocalypse, however, but about the Surrealist technique of poetic invention. His early poetry, more vague and incoherent than that of Thomas, Treece, or Gascoyne, baffled critics. In *Auden and After* (1942), Francis Scarfe concludes, "I can make nothing of the poems of Norman McCaig, whose only modification of the surrealist-catalogue poem is that he divides it up into stanzas of equal length."[3]

MacCaig's first of "Nine Poems" in *The White Horseman* represents in part a curious Surrealistic fusion of infectious apocalyptic imagery and romantic "love" poetry, although Eluard in "La Mame de Carseau" had earlier linked love and end-of-the-world thinking. MacCaig's apocalyptic images signal not the end of the world, but the end of love. They suggest, through aggressive phallic symbolism, a symbolic assault on an unwilling, cold paramour: MacCaig brings to his love not flowers, but "elephants," with presumable Freudian trunks; a "eucalyptus tree" on or in a possibly circular island; a military "fleet of ships"; "a complete alp"; "volcano tops"; and a "massive trumpet." Vertically erect, rocklike, or huge, such symbols intimate phallic size and condition and, by implication, male sexual potency. His potentially erupting volcano and "angelic saliva" as a consequence of heaven's "fall in a massive trumpet sound" suggest as well semen and orgasm:

> I brought you elephants and volcano tops
> and a eucalyptus tree on a coral island,
> I had them in baskets. You looked with surprise
> and went away to pick weeds out of the ground.
> I brought you under my arm a fleet of ships
> and a complete alp and you went and gardened.
> Now heaven fall in a massive tumpet sound
>
> and scuttle your crab head under its angelic saliva.

Failing to appease his unresponsive paramour, MacCaig or his persona finds in the apocalyptic emphasis on judgment, or judgment day with angelic trumpet in conventional language, a means of imaginatively bringing to judgment his unresponsive mistress.

MacCaig's volcano image is interesting inasmuch as it suggests the sense of impending doom in apocalyptic poetry metamorphosed into biological, sexual mounting tension seeking orgasmic release. Apocalyptic climax to history, similarly, becomes symbolically connected to sexual climax in orgasm.

Under the influence of Freud and the Surrealists, MacCaig and some of the Neo-Romantics link sex and aggression, Freud's two dominant instincts. But earlier Romantics, such as Blake in "The Immortal" and Coleridge in "Kubla Khan," also provide models by ambiguously intimating that sexual and aggressive instincts are linked and may be dangerously repressed, like the contents of a volcano: Coleridge's "Ancestral voices prophesying war!" and "fast thick pants" preliminary to his fountain's eruption, and Blake's "Prophetic wrath, struggling for vent" that "heaves" with "bursting sobs." Nearer in time, Barker implies sexual climax in his "Elegy No. I" about war, while suggesting a cosmic apocalypse:

> . . . on this occasion Time
> Swells like a wave at a wall and bursts to eternity.
> I await when the engine of lilies and lakes and love
> Reaching its peak of power blows me sky high, and I
>   Come down to rest
> On the shape I made in the ground where I used to lie.

The volcano is the appropriate symbol of the psyche for Barker, MacCaig, Thomas, and Moore (as in Moore's imagery of "Taut Volcanoes/Ready to Explode" in "Happy without Sex"). Following Freud, they generally accepted a nineteenth-century hydraulic model of the psyche as a closed energy system analogous to that of a steam engine. Unsublimated instincts will explode if thoroughly repressed.

Two years after the publication of MacCaig's "Nine Poems" in *The White Horseman*, his first volume of poetry, *Far Cry* (1943) was published. In it MacCaig's Surrealistic suspension of the laws of causation creates poetry which is dreamlike in texture or on the verge of madness: "The hare of reason runs, my dewy girl," MacCaig writes, "and birds go mad in bushes."[4] Surrealistic suspension of causation's laws also expresses the frightening and unsafe environments within the mind and without in a world torn by war. Terror is a dominant ingredient of MacCaig's universe—the "terror of storm," the "terror of ocean," and the "terror and chain of unreason."[5]

MacCaig's unfocused collages in *Far Cry* echo the cosmic imagery of Surrealism and occasionally the visionary and judgmental imagery of the biblical Apocalypse. MacCaig presents agents of impending retribution, generated internally by the superego, as Greek "private harpies" (cf. Sartre's *The Flies*, published the same year) joined by Christian messengers of judgment, "archangels" and "Gabriels." A judgment-day "universal trumpet" which ushers again into history the "immaculate messiah" reinforces the retributive character of MacCaig's vision:

From the light that breeds in the overhead sky

one vision, transmitted in nerves
and distilled in the talking vault of a skull,
is used to crowd the air with private harpies
archangels angels cherubims Gabriels.
A mood's moment chirping in the hairy shell
of a sickened ear fills the sky's waves

with the piercing universal trumpet,
the golden tongue braying of guilt and blood
or the fanfare usher of an immaculate messiah.[6]

The psychology of MacCaig's early poetry, although ambiguously presented, is conventional enough to allow interpretation. In *Far Cry,* oscillations between terror and joy are metamorphosed into depression in manic-depressive fashion. Action and agitation in *Far Cry* are similarly replaced by emotional exhaustion. MacCaig, who arrives at an emotional state in which he sits, "Only with dull eyes/watching . . . a dreary sea depositing/its doleful lumps of water on a dead beach" is anticipated by Coleridge, who more lucidly in his "Dejection: An Ode" sinks into inactivity in "dull pain" and "drowsy, unimpassioned grief," complaining, "And still I gaze—and with how blank an eye!" MacCaig's "dreary sea" and "dead beach" are projections of subjective states into external, or objective, reality. They are like Ruskin's "storm-cloud of the nineteenth century" and Coleridge's dead, "inanimate cold world," a product, as Coleridge recognizes, of the imagination which can give "life" and "light" to external reality: ". . . a fair luminous cloud/Enveloping the Earth. . . ." The desirable alternative for Coleridge is "Joy" and for MacCaig, "rapture." But the degree of faith in the individual's power to self-generate emotional states has waned. MacCaig's world, like that of Sartre, Kafka, Hemingway, West, and other writers treating anxiety-depression, is less well-lighted, darker, less hopeful.

MacCaig in *Far Cry* also treats the modern paralysis of the will, abulia, caused less by excess or satiation than by deprivation, "this lack of living." The solution for abulia MacCaig announces in the first poem of the sequence: "The crying courage that has wolves running in it is the only courage that outlasts a wave falling. . . ." But the poet, less wolf-like in courage, finds himself "sitting spiritless, a tick-tocking shadow,"[8] on whom the emptiness of human existence weighs heavily.[9] Paralysis of will in *Far Cry* is also a reaction to a world dissolving, "the colourless collapse of nation upon nation,"[10] "dissolving beauty,"[11] and dissolving Surrealistic environment of "unscalable moons/dissolving in fire."[12]

In "Poetry Today" Charles Tomlinson argues that MacCaig, whose poetry is included in Alvarez's *The New Poetry,* "is the one poet who survived from the New Apocalypse to write verse which, in its narrow but intense way, exhibits both a sense of philosophic comedy and a craggy integrity."[13] That MacCaig's later poetry is decidedly post-

Apocalyptic is also Helmstadter's conclusion.[14] MacCaig himself has commented on his progression not away from the New Apocalypse, but away from Surrealism: "I was fascinated by the way surrealism allowed the imagination a freedom amounting to promiscuity and it took me a long time to escape from it," he explains.[15] As a poet he moves toward a more ordered, controlled, realistic, ironic, and conversational and philosophical mode of expression.

"No Escape" in *Riding Lights* (1956) more economically and directly expresses some of the Surrealist sexual aggressiveness against women which characterizes MacCaig's "Nine Poems."[16] But in "Birds All Singing," MacCaig in effect finishes the destruction of the nineteenth-century Romantic symbol of the bird, as in Shelley's "To a Skylark," begun by Hardy in "The Darkling Thrush." Neither harbinger of doom nor divine instructor, as in Treece's "Pastoral," the bird sings simply because of its territorial instinct.[17]

Read viewed Surrealism as one manifestation of Romanticism. From such a perspective, MacCaig's early verse may be considered Romantic. But MacCaig sees himself as more Classical than Romantic and, as to the New Apocalypse, notes that he never agreed to its manifesto or editorial statements.[18]

G. S. Fraser

The "main aims" of the Apocalyptic Movement "have been fairly completely expressed by the main leaders, Henry Treece, G. S. Fraser and J. F. Hendry," writes Francis Scarfe in *Auden and After*.[19] Hendry, however, has recently noted that Tom Scott, a Scottish poet associated with the Apocalyptic group, "can verify . . . that in fact I dictated the Apocalyptic manifesto; and later even the Introduction to *The White Horseman,* to G. S. Fraser, who knew little of what was going on and was himself rather Neo-Augustan."[20]

Fraser himself, as Paddy Fraser notes, "got slightly tired of the 'Apocalypse' label later on."[21] Like Nicholas Moore and Norman MacCaig, he came to disassociate himself from the Apocalyptic Movement. His aesthetic and philosophical perspective is probably nearest to that of Moore, with whom Fraser maintained a "close" "literary relationship."[22]

After the war, Fraser announced in *Three Philosophical Essays* that he has been influenced by "French philosophers, like Gabriel Marcel, Jean-Paul Sartre, and Albert Camus. . . ."[23] Existentialism coalesces with Fraser's lingering Neo-Romanticism in his conclusion that "every human life" should be considered as a "unique project, a striving towards completeness. . . ."[24] The distance between Fraser and the New Apocalypse in particular is evident, however, in Fraser's argument,

> though it is a merit for a writer to have a style that expresses his personality, it is still greater merit for him to have one that transcends it. . . . In really great writing, in prose or verse, the writer's personality becomes like a transparency; it is the medium through which we see something else, of much greater importance.[25]

Fraser's line of reasoning recalls Eliot's Neo-Classical conclusion that poetry involves "not the expression of personality" but its "extinction," and that "the poet has, not a 'personality to express,' but a particular medium . . . in which impressions and experiences combine in peculiar and unexpected ways."[26]

Fraser, whose "Inside Story" appears in Treece and Schimanski's first *Transformation* anthology, also writes of "personalism." But his approach to what he calls the "rather vague philosophy called 'personalism' " is more the product of Marcel and Sartre than of Treece and Schimanski (cf. Treece's Personalism, Chapter 5), although Fraser, like Treece and Hendry, is influenced by Read, who, Fraser notes,

> . . . has made a distinction, useful within limits, between the notions of personality and character: character being what is fixed and reliable, but therefore on the whole uncreative, personality being what is fluid and responsive, in human nature.[27]

Fraser's postwar thinking fuses Read and Sartre. Echoing both, he argues that the concept of "person" is "more concrete" than that of a man or woman as "an individual."[28] Moreover, "character in a sense is potentiality, where personality is achievement."[29] Existentialism's emphasis on the concrete, existing person is at work, as is Sartre's judgment that only in concrete, actual achievements is the individual defined.

Never as preoccupied with terror as Hendry, MacCaig, Barker, or

Treece, Fraser concludes, "One's doubts about Existentialism . . . have to do chiefly with the suggestion that the indivdual [*sic*] is more real to himself in a state of distance and dread, facing a void."[30] Like Abraham Maslow, Fraser wants to keep the wheat of Existentialism while discarding what he sees as its superfluous negative chaff. Moreover, paraphrasing Sartre, Fraser arrives at a position close to Third Force psychologists such as Maslow and Carl Rogers on the inherent unknowability of the self. His line of reasoning recalls Heisenberg's uncertainty principle, in which subatomic particles cannot be observed since photons, necessary for illumination, displace them:

We can never properly know even the self that *can* be observed; each attempt to know it transforms its nature. When I try to analyse a feeling, what I arrive at the end of the analysis is something less genuine and impressive than what I started with. It is not quite the same thing; it has withered or shrunk.

All this is true, yet it is doubtful whether it justifies such a morose attitude as Sartre's or whether its practical outcome may not be merely to warn us against excessive introspection.[31]

In other words, Existentialism provides additional reasons for rejecting, among other things, Apocalyptic and Surrealistic preoccupation with plumbing the depths of the psyche.

Rather than self-absorption, Fraser argues that "the personality that charms us is the almost unconscious expressing of a devotion to something beyond it." He cites Marcel, who notes that the "human self . . . is a screen, not a projector. It is not our source of light."[32] But of course in Romantic theory, as H. M. Abrams so ably demonstrated in his *The Mirror and the Lamp*, published shortly after Fraser's book of essays, the self is a "projector"[33] and source of light. Abrams notes that it was Plotinus, who analogized the creative mind to a "radiating sun," who was "the chief begetter of the archetype of the projector; and both the romantic theory of knowledge and the romantic theory of poetry can be accounted the remote descendants of this root-image of Plotinian philosophy."[34] Fraser follows Marcel in concluding that self-knowledge is a product of disinterested knowledge of others. Our sense of "personal reality," Fraser notes that Marcel taught, arises not from our attempts at introspection but from our bonds with others. It is when we are so absorbed in others as to forget ourselves that we are at the same time real.[35]

But Fraser does not come to a Christian Existentialist position. Rather, he reaffirms what he calls our "common tradition" which emphasizes "reason" and "rational argument." In a manner more reminiscent of logical positivism than of Existentialism or Apocalypticism, Fraser argues that "probably the duty of the intellectual to-day is not so much to suggest conclusions that might bring it [the debate through which a "wider version of truth may emerge"] to an end as to clarify the terms in which it is conducted."[36] Truth is, in other words, a product of the marketplace of ideas, a liberal vision of the dialectics of establishing truth, after the manner of John Stuart Mill and Walter Lippmann. Truth is not the private truth of Kierkegaard or the private myth of the Apocalyptics.

Poetry. Some of Fraser's poems treat Existentialist perspectives. His "The Human Condition," for example, reflects the emphasis in Existentialism on defining not a common human nature, but a common human condition or predicament. But Fraser's position sounds more like a blend of Hardy's cautious meliorism tinged with religious hope than like Sartre or Camus: "I promise nothing. But I say / That we can know a better way / And may have grace to follow it. . . ."[37] Like Sartre, Fraser treats the necessity for a mode of existence that transcends self-deception and includes choice and inescapable anxiety as part of the human condition:

> Yes, the case is what it is.
> There is dignity in this,
> In choosing to be not deceived. . . .
>
> Language has its uses then
> In differentiating men
> From less anxious animal. . . .[38]

But in place of commitment, despair, or the courage to be, Fraser recommends a temperate hope: "Do not hope for safety, but / At the worst remember that / None are saved who lose their hope."[39]

His title recalls that of Spender's "The Human Situation" and Thomas Gunn's "Human Condition," which appears in the first volume of Robert Conquest's anti-Romantic *New Lines* (1956). Gunn's poem is as didactic and prosaic as Fraser's, but reflects Camus's agnosticism and Heidegger's emphasis on intellectual finitude. Rather than condemned to freedom, as in Sartre, the poet or his persona is "condemned to be/An individual," which involves for Gunn a Heideggerian or Pateresque recognition of our inescapable and intellectually limiting isolation from the psychic inner worlds of others. Fog, indicating the unavoidable cloudiness of reason and our perspective of external reality, rather than darkness, becomes for Gunn the appropriate metaphor. Stylistically, also, both Fraser's "The Human Situation" and Gunn's "Human Condition" represent amalgams in which a prewar view of poetry as a vehicle for exploring ideas, rather than the unconscious, fuses with postwar inquisitiveness about European Existentialism.

Fraser himself notes in his *Leaves Without a Tree* that his poetry gains its "conversational diction" from Auden, as well as Pope, Byron, and "parts of Browning."[40] Some Augustan qualities, also at work in the later poems of Comfort, are at work in Fraser's relatively nonmetaphoric "A Letter to Nicholas Moore":

> But you, my friend, I think were always loved
> Were always lucky in the natural mode
> And now your luck has turned to certainty:
> That was the impulse by which I was moved
> Before the horse ran that I thought I rode—
> To order flowers to your felicity.[41]

In other respects, the poem reflects Fraser's aversion to excessive introspection and immoderate, florid, tangled, and obscure imagery in poetry. His own more prosaic, rational poetry lacks those qualities, and his objections to such Apocalyptic qualities in poetry foreshadow those of the *New Lines* poets of the 1950s. Fraser writes, "Let me be sane and sensible and flat."[42]

But among the early poems there are interesting exceptions, such as Fraser's "Crisis." It is a quasi-apocalyptic dream vision with Anglo Saxon–like pronouncements, such as "Then came sorrow":

My room as usual a disorder of books,
Nothing to my hand, my clothes flung on a chair,
My desk squalid and fussy with useless papers,
I had shut myself up from the clean shock of day.
I was asleep: Like a criminal, without dreams.
There was nothing I desired but my own pride.

Then it seemed to me the earth opened,
I was on a green slope, an unsafe hillside,
With rocks there and rivers; there was that lady
And one man, my enemy. We three clung together
And rolled down the hill. The river whelmed,
I gripped her greedily. Then came sorrow.
She was not with me, I drowned alone:
That man mocked on the bank

    I almost awakened,
But sorrow and sleep together bind fast
Falling far, I came to a strange city,
No one knew me, I walked in sorrow alone.
Past smoke-black brick and yellow muslin curtains,
Vainly round interminable corners,
For these streets were familiar and not familiar
(The old tenements of Glasgow and my childhood)
And I knew I would never find my own house.[43]

Fraser's "Crisis" had a spiritual guide or ghostly visitant, as in Treece's "To the Edge and Back." But in Fraser's poem he has become a doppelgänger.

Spiritual guides in poetry may be interpreted in a number of ways. In the Freudian-dominated 1930s and 1940s, the spiritual guide may distantly reflect the conventional image of the analyst as a paternal, authoritarian figure who guides the analysand through the unconscious to the edge of madness and back or Jung's wise old man who communicates superior insight and intuition. Yet he may represent as well a part of the personality from which the poet-seer feels alienated or is becoming alienated, as in Barker's "Resolution of Dependence" in which appears a resurrected Wordsworth.

The task of the post-seer in such cases is to understand the neglected part of his personality which the visitant embodies: in the case of Barker's Wordsworth, individualism and Romantic rebellion against mass conformity. Where the ghostly visitant is a doppelgänger or double, the task required again may be to incorporate within the self the alienated or neglected attitude, as in Barker's "Epistle I," in which the double represents compassion, or as in Comfort's "Sixth Elegy," in which the double represents death consciousness. On the other hand, the task may be to reintegrate the self on a new basis which excludes an unworthy or detrimental personality characteristic. Fraser or his persona in "Crisis" becomes aware of a part of himself which is a social mask reflecting the demand of society for conformity. Struggling for a more genuine mode of existence which may involve creating tensions in the social order, Fraser feels betrayed by his socially conforming, Existentially inauthentic alter ego. Attaining wholeness for a life "all in bits" means, by implication, developing a more authentic, less externally directed, mode of existence:

> Then I met myself in my dream, I said clearly,
> "I am going soon, take care of yourself, find friends."
> But my own eyes looked through me, my voice said, "Traitor!"
> And I saw then
> All the terrible company of the defeated,
> Lost but in the courage of shapes of stone:
> The stone mouths of the rigid orators. . . .
> Then I awoke, sweating: I came out to the window,
> In the evening light saw the snow grey on the ground.
> I turned to my darkening room, I saw my papers
> Scattered about, my life too lately
> Had been all in bits. "My God," I said, "there is something
> Far wrong, certainly, somewhere. But with me or the world?"

Fraser's vision of "All the terrible company of the defeated" recalls the imagery of other apocalyptic visions: Hendry's "multitudinous, armies of humanity,/Wondering over vestal victories" in *The Orchestral Mountain;* "half-a-million sufferers" in Treece's "To the Edge and Back"; Barker's "visitation of the conspicuously dead,/Terrifying me with their mad pageantry" in "Vision of England '38"; and Eliot's "hooded hordes swarming/Over endless plains . . ." in *The Waste Land.*

To some extent the appearance of seemingly limitless crowds of people in the poetry of the 1930s and 1940s probably reflects newsreel footage of mass Fascist rallies, such as those held yearly in Nuremberg by the Nazis, as well as newsreel footage of refugees in mass migrations across the plains of Europe. Moreover, compassion for the "mass of man," in Barker's language, becomes projected in images of mass crowds, which express as well fear of the dehumanized, depersonalized amorphous masses in which the individual may lose his personal identity. But such imagery also echoes earlier apocalyptic literature, such as St. John's vision of the hundred and forty-four thousand; Langland's "fair field full of folke" in *Piers Plowman;* the Pearl Poet's dream of the "flawless company . . . /Of thousand massed, so great a throng"; and Shelley's vision in "The Triumph of Life" of a "pageant" or "great stream/Of people . . . hurrying to and fro,/Numerous as gnats," and "All hastening onward. . . ."

Nicholas Moore

Biographical Perspectives. According to Gardiner, Moore's poetry is "extremely romantic," although Moore, like Levertov, never would have thought of himself "as a Neo-Romantic."[44] Hoffman and Scarfe view Moore as one of the "British poets," in Hoffman's language, "who called themselves the 'Poets of the Apocalypse.' . . ."[45]

From a biographical viewpoint, Nicholas Moore is perhaps the most interesting writer associated with the New Apocalypse and Neo-Romanticism. His father was the famous philosopher G. E. Moore. "My father was very much a philosopher's philosopher," Moore writes, citing such works of his father as "A Defence of Common-Sense," *The Refutation of Idealism,* and "Proofs of an External World."[46] Moore sees no direct relationship between his poetry and his father's views, although he acknowledges that his father's "ideas must have influenced" him to some degree in his upbringing.[47] But it is probably Moore's acceptance of his father's general philosophical perspective combined with his own lack of interest in finding a Weltanschauung which partly accounts for his antipathy toward the mystical, transcendental perspective of Hendry and Treece, as well as

Moore's lack of interest in Treece's artistic escape from ordinary experience and the introspective focus of much Neo-Romantic poetry, such as that of Thomas and Wrey Gardiner.

In most respects, Moore had a fortunate upbringing. For holidays, his father often took his family to Southwold, renting a bungalow by the sea. Nearby, the Freuds had a converted barn. "Freud, the son of *the* Freud, was an architect," Moore recalls, with a "beautiful raven-haired browned-skinned wife" and a son, Lucian, the artist, with whom Moore played. Lucian was later to illustrate Moore's *The Glass Tower.* As well as being a philosopher, G. E. Moore "of course was a great influence on what is now known as Bloomsbury and the Bloomsbury group, and his personal friends ranged far outside academic philosophy" to include "the Trevelyans, G. M., the historian, a fellow O. M., and Bob, the poet, a particular friend," Leonard and Virginia Woolf, Lytton Strachey, Sidney Keyes, Rupert Brooke, A. E. Housman, Desmond McCarthy, and others. As a result, "there was a wide-angling intellectual atmosphere, though not oppressively so that I remember,"[48] Moore recalls.

Like his father's visitors, his mother "was very garrulous." Moore writes that she was also "inclined both to boast about me embarrassingly and inaccurately to her acquaintances and to run me down to myself, my father, and to some of her closest friends, so much so that they used, when they could get a word in, to protest." By contrast, his "father, who was always smiling to himself, who loved puns and had his own sense of humour—he used to slap his forehead and shout 'silly billy,' when he was thinking he's made a mistake about something—whether a deep philosophical question or a trivial household task—was a very mild man, not easily roused to wrath—though it was terrible on the few occasions it came. . . ."[49]

Both parents "read literature." His father was fond of those "mostly among his contemporaries, more or less": Tennyson, Arnold, Wordsworth, Thomas Hood, Edward Lear, Trollope, and Jane Austen. "Some of these," Moore writes, "he used to read aloud to my mother, and Lear and Lewis Carroll he used to read to us children." His mother was "something of an official expert on children's books," and, as a result, the children were also "brought up on Hugh Lofting and Doctor Doolittle of recent Newley-Push-Me-Pull-You fame." Also, his mother, although "not an active suffragette," was "always strong for women's rights and equality for women," as well as "the most modern ideas current in children's education and indeed with the seething new intellectual life of the times." Moore and his brother, a composer and musician, went to the "very new progressive school Dartington Hall," having both previously gone to "The Dragon School Oxford (of which John Betjeman, incidentally, was also earlier a pupil)." His first "real interest in poetry" was "brought about by a good English master called Brown," and, Moore adds, "I remember being very pleased with a translation I made at that slender age of Heidenroslein."[50]

Moore's uncle was Thomas Sturge Moore. His "aesthetic theories were tosh" and his prose style "undoubtedly unreadable," thought G. E. Moore, who "was fond of quoting to us children with great delight the poem of Uncle Tom's which went, 'How nice it is to eat,/ All creatures love it so.' " Although the poem was intended for children, Moore's father "quoted it with obvious relish and clearly thought it extremely (unconsciously) funny." "Uncle Tom had no sense of humour and a great sense of his own importance and high seriousness," Moore concludes, adding,

I'm sure T. Sturge Moore was in deadly earnest. But I think we all thought about him—though of course my father was very fond of him and he had an awfully majestic poetic appearance (the trouble is he had a very thin rather namby-pamby precise little voice to go with it)—as Gavin Ewart has expressed it in a recent small poem:

> When I was young
> I found T. Sturge Moore
> a very boring poet—
> But now that I am old
> I find him even more boring still.

—a sentiment with which I must concur, though as a dutiful nephew, when young I did do my very utmost to see some good in him.[51]

Beyond the humor of it all, the attitude of Moore and his father to T. S. Moore has relevance to Moore's attitude toward the New Apocalypse. Humor, wit, and irony are not characteristics of the Apocalyptic art of Treece and Hendry, and Moore's personal reaction to

Treece and Hendry was probably in part negative because of their
analogous attitude of "high seriousness."

Moore took more seriously the poetry of Wallace Stevens. "I did
have some correspondence with Stevens and held him in high re-
gard," Moore writes. "Unfortunately I used to carry his letters in my
wallet, and it was pinched by a pickpocket in Petticoat Lane." The
thief got "letters from Wallace Stevens and Osbert Sitwell and a few
bills." Moore also acknowledges "going through a short Thomas
phase—but it was nothing like Thomas." He especially admired
Thomas's "The Map of Love" and *The Portrait of the Artist as a Young
Dog.* He also was "attracted to Barker's early writings" and likes
"Calamiteeror very much, and his long 'Spain' poem."[52]

Three of Moore's poems are included by Hendry in *The New Apocalypse.* In a letter of 24 August 1940 to Treece about *The White Horseman,* Hendry writes, "I suggest . . . for the creative side: *you, me,
Moore.* . . ." Twelve of Moore's poems appear in *The White Horseman.*
But the relationship between Moore and Hendry, in particular, had
become increasingly strained. Writing to Treece on 8 March 1939,
Goodland had noted, "Moore probably won't like the Hendry poems.
This is a warning!" Reminiscing, Hendry believes that "Moore was
unhappy that Goodland had any ideas on his own and tried always to
manipulate us, as he had through Goodland."[53] But such a conclusion
does not take into account that Moore did not share Goodland's enthusiasm for finding a "Weltanschauung."

Moore and Alex Comfort were two of the "three 'stars' of a school-
boy's poetry anthology called *The Threshold.*"[54] They also knew each
other as fellow students at Cambridge, and, later, at Gardiner's Grey
Walls Press. Moore "had a large toothy smile like the Great Pump-
kin," Comfort remembers, "and a gorgeous live-in girl-friend Priscilla with long dark hair."[55] Much of Moore's poetry is dedicated to
Priscilla.

Besides *Seven,* Moore considered for a while starting up another
magazine—"a magazine for our generation" with the help of two
friends, Jack Bayliss and Newton.[56] In a letter of 20 January 1942 to
Comfort, Moore writes of the proposed magazine that it "will, perhaps, be called the Fortune Anthology, and we've persuaded Caton of
the Fortune Press to produce a second number, if we get the money

for the first. . . ." Moore adds that the magazine is "not specifically
an apocalyptic magazine—but, of course, I am in with it, and we
hope to print some not well-enough-known Americans with it." Edited by Bayliss, Newton, and Moore, *The Fortune Anthology* was published once by Caton in 1942.

In answering a question on what was Apocalyptic enough about
Moore to include him in the Apocalyptic anthologies, Hendry has replied, "His 'innocence,' " an innocence which Hendry also finds at
work in the paintings of Cecil Collins.[57] More unarguably, Moore,
like Treece, Hendry, Comfort, Bayliss, Keyes, Stanford, and Gardiner, writes in reaction to the Auden group, although his objections
to them do not run as deeply. Both Barker and Thomas had "a pa-
nache and an attitude to words" that Moore liked. "One of my other
discontents with the previous generation," Moore writes, "was their
dryness of language, absence of rhodomontade or rhetoric of fine language. Thomas and Barker had these elements."[58] And what was or
is his major difference from the Apocalyptics? Moore observes,

. . . the greatest difference between my ideas and those of the apocalyptics
[is] that a lot of my writing is ironic, but often taken by others as deadly
serious—or a jape at some other style or belief—and may mean, from my
point of view, the direct opposite of what it says.[59]

Poetry. "The Ruin and the Sun" in *The White Horseman* is the
longest of Moore's poems to be anthologized by Hendry. Like Read's
"Bombing Casualties in Spain," Auden's "Spain," or Spender's "Fall
of a City," Moore's poem laments the Spanish Civil War: "O Spain,
whose vineyards have run with blood." Moore's style manifests some
of the "rhetoric of fine language" which he finds lacking in the poetry
of the Auden group, but the poem is more memorable for its narrator's imaginative and emotional identification with the victims of
war's slaughter.

Contrasting himself to the Auden group, Moore notes, "I was
never exactly disillusioned [with Communism] because I never had
any illusions except possibly in thinking that a better world and a
better system might come about, which didn't."[60] Such a hope characterizes the perspectives of the personae in both "The Ruin and the

Sun" and "Who See the Coming of the Morning." Transcending private myth or "personal symbol," the speaker in the later poem envisions a "revolution" based in human solidarity:

> For still beyond the personal symbol
> In the morning we reach out to a world,
> Not content with a single word,
> But one word that speaks for all the people,
> O I have been at the birth of Venus.
>
> With the coming of the morning
> More will come than our personal song,
> But it will be a part of the people's
> The revolution in the world
> That makes a star more than a star.

Moore's persona in "A Salutation for Theodore Dreiser" finds
Dreiser—whose novels grimly present the Capitalist system—and
Paul Robeson—the black American actor, singer, football star, and
political activist—champions of the proletarian underdog:

> From London, Liverpool, or the high peak of Scotland,
> Wherever people gather to talk about the world,
> Thankful for your voice and for the voice of Paul Robeson,
> They take courage in their torment, hope in their anguish,
> Ready to see love extinguish the sharp fires of Fascism.
>
> Ready to accept the American voice that is not willed by
>   Wall Street,
> Of a great writer or singer, who speak out for the people.

A sense of personal impending doom is at work in Moore's "Epistle
to H. T. (for Henry Treece)," which treats the fear of Anne Frank–
like arrest and detention or conscription, but probably not Moore's.
"I was a pacifist in the war, possibly the only one to be given exemption by the Tribunal purely on moral grounds (i.e., not religious or
belonging to organizations against whose principles it was, etc., or
any of the usual reasons for which exemption was sought)," Moore
observes.[61] Sounding like Auden in "The Quarry," Moore's persona
complains of the "incalculable terror" and wishes "not to be hurt by

the military knock on the door." His anxiety and despair, more dis-
organizing than Hardy's or Sartre's before an impersonal universe, reflect the private reactions of countless others at the time: in particular, a generalized sense of individual will not being able to alter the
course of events:

> Tonight I am Lear, a mad young image of Hamlet.
> I hear and fear the waves of tomorrow's sea,
> Not knowing what in their will will become of me.
> I can only offer them a skull, and my hand.

Moore's persona in "Nostalgia" expresses disillusionment with a
postwar world which fails to satisfy his desire for a significantly im-
proved world. His Grecian soldier recalls Ulysses returning to Ithaca
to find Penelope besieged by suitors or Sartre's Orestes coming to
Argos. Beginning with a Freudian symbol of sexual potency, "a
bronze spear," the poem ends with descriptions of psychological and
social impotency and despair.

> I see a bowman, and the hunted beast. . . .
> The bronze spear hangs symbolic over me. . . .
> To return home, to return
> To what used to be.
>
> To return to Argos. . . .
>
> To return and find the people not slaves,
> The castle walls not covered with moss. . . .
>
> I return and read
> In the newspapers new cunnings,
> Of new tyrants, new defeats,
> Strikes, lockouts, prisoners, crime. . . .
>
> I have returned
> To Argos, and I find my wife the mistress
> Of a new lover. The wars are over,
> The people are free. Yet what is that to me?
> I am met again even here by the same lie.[62]

Some of Moore's poems treat love and lust, for which he has been criticized; Francis Scarfe argues tenuously that many of Moore's poems "fail" because "they are unpleasantly exhibitionist: 'I still remember, darling, the warmth of your legs.' "[63] In "The Mountain and the Valley (for Priscilla)" Moore exploits flower and topographical sexual symbolism in an unusually blatant depiction, considering the decade in which it was written, of female fascination with the male sexual organ (the phallic-shaped "pink, pointed orchid" or "flower" "between my legs/, . . . your kissed/And precious symbol"), intercourse, and orgasm (". . . you are/The green valley coaxing the rills from the mountain").[64]

Included by Comfort in Treece and Schimanski's *A New Romantic Anthology*, Moore's "Prayer to Nobody, Who Is Something (for Priscilla)" recalls Auden's "Sir, no man's enemy" in "Petition." In Moore's poem, Moses' burning "bush" and "dry sticks" become Thomasesque female pubic hair and genitalia, and the poet must "die" for seeing God or female genitalia, or "die" in sexual orgasm, as in metaphysical poetry:

> Dear Sir and Father, I have been praying. . . .
> It was February and the year was young, the sun . . .
>
> Was scarcely hot enough to taste, and her eyes
> Pulled me down among the dry sticks and the frozen snow,
> Lifted up her belly like a bottle to my gaze,
> That there below I should see a bush and die.

Moore's irreverent poem allows also his heavenly "Father" to be interpreted as the earthly father of an Oedipally anxious son who attempts to escape condemnation by confessing all or going public. The poem's title recalls Blake's God of institutionalized religion, "Nobodaddy," who, from a Freudian perspective, is a projection of the earthly father.

In "The Hair's Breadth," also included in *A New Romantic Anthology*, Moore's persona again fuses mistress and Deity to express conventional Western confusion over the role of women. Moore's Barkeresque pun on "Dog," which spelled in reverse is "God," expresses such confusion about women who, barred from equality, are to be either dominated or pedestalized and fawningly worshiped:

> Tell me, hair of her head, where should I lie
> Who wish to praise her in my poetry?
> Tell me, hair of her thigh, what should I do
> Who wish to make my image of her true?
>
> Dog by the lamp-post, God above the clouds,
> Am I to follow either with my words?
> Is she a bitch to be by flesh accosted,
> Or holy image and by blood attested?

"Lovers Under the Elms" begins with epigraphs from Sartre and John Wilmot, Earl of Rochester ("Nothing! thou elder brother ev'n to Shade"). Also personifying nothingness, Moore's persona declares,

> Nothing comes like a faint prick under the eyelids
> Or a trick played on one by one's enemy;
> Nothing becomes a giant, but is nowhere
> In the air or sea or sky:
>
> Is disease, despair, incalculable misfortune,
> The line drawn thin between two lovers. . . .

In *Existence and Being* Heidegger argues that dread *(Angst)* may suddenly reveal "Nothing," which is not an object and, therefore, heretofore ignored by science. Yet nothingness is at the core of one's being. In *Being and Nothingness,* Sartre, influenced by Heidegger, argues that the "existence of desire as a human fact is sufficient to prove that human reality is a lack."[65] Similarly, Moore's persona asserts that Nothing

> comes like a sudden cancer
> Or a long spell of cold and snow,
> Is always between one's hope, the lack in one's being;
> Exists, and does not go. . . .[66]

The psychic revelation for Heidegger, Sartre, and Moore's persona in "Lovers Under the Elms" is of nothingness or nonbeing which inescapably permeates being.

Heideggerian nothingness is also the subject of "Suitable Emotions," in which Moore's persona attempts to ward off dread, the "suitable" response to a confrontation with nothingness, by engaging the inhibitory emotions of ironic detachment. Since nothing, as defined by Heidegger, functions as a presence which must be encountered, but is not a subject which exists, Moore can use the word "nothing" in several puns: "But alas! there is Nothing to stand behind her," "There is Nothing—for which I need to be consoled," et cetera:

> I, too, saw Nothing, standing by the door,
> A sombre and hooded figure, Mr. X, . . .
>
> Everything ends in an X. There is nothing more. . . .
>
> For he does not live or exist at all in a way,
> This sinister X, this man of mystery. . . .
>
> He is the dark protagonist of a fable
> Which you know in your heart is inescapable. . . .
>
> You know it's all happened already. And, as you wait,
> Your darling appears. She has a smile on her face,
> But alas! there is Nothing to stand behind her, gaunt
> And crooked. She does not see, but waves and beckons
> In a suitable fashion. It's just as you might have to
>   reckon.
>
> I know my loss, and what I have lost is not Nothing.
> Nothing remains behind, and with slow attrition
> Eats away till the dream becomes a horror. . . .
> I look at Nothing beside my chair with loathing,
> But refrain from showing too suitable an emotion.
> I would melt to the ground like a pillar of salt in terror.
> But have learnt to keep a kind of detached control.
> There is Nothing—for which I need to be consoled—
> But at least there is you who may, if I'm clever, console.[67]

In "Ode to Fear," Moore's persona personifies and addresses emotions, somewhat after the manner of Neo-Classical writers addressing abstractions. Finding in the ode an appropriate vehicle to express the pathos of his condition, he finds, as well, that fear of consequences inhibits the gratification of human needs and aspirations. As such, it is a cause of the mental disease which the Apocalyptics and the Neo-Romantics generally thought they could cure: the fragmentation of the self into warring entities:

> Before you, adamant Fear,
> Bully and dictator, creator of self-division,
> Flayer of true passion![68]

In "Recollection," Moore treats stone figures in relief on a frieze, figures in varying copulatory positions, as in Hindu temple art, which the poem, like MacNeice's "Mahabalipuram," may describe. But a more likely point of departure may have been Keat's "Ode on a Grecian Urn." Both poems treat the apparent endlessly unconsummated sexual desire of sculptured figures in works of art:

> I recall the photographs, the stone limbs caught
> In every sexual attitude, the carved
> And inane figures frozen in their frieze.
> Never to accomplish their desire,
> But to hold always to the half-performed!
> How vain their sensual attitudes! How they must tire
> Of holding forever each aesthetic pose,
> Stone-cold, their faces set
> In immobile resignation, never to be warmed
> By the real fire, . . .
> I recall, too, words written in vain,
> Vain tones, as when I wrote
> "I love your breasts they look so firm"
> Or "I want to have salacious you
> Alone and naked in a bed,"
> Lines from a doggerel poem,
> As though a letter, from which one might quote
> Half-a-dozen words; but again
> It is all cold, something we never do,
> Something which will remain
> In the dry letter or a flame puffed out in the head.
> A reminiscence of unaccomplished beauty or pain.[69]

Concerning "The Indian and the Shark," which begins with a declaration that "Politics is not poetry," Moore has commented: ". . . I am saying in effect 'That has become the accepted view—but it isn't true.' "[70] Like MacNeice in "Not Entirely," Moore in "The Indian and the Shark" attacks either-or mentality, specifically that of political and literary movements, whether Marxist and Classical or anarchist and Romantic. The fragmented world is redeemed by poetry which transcends narrow conceptualizations:

> An Indian went swimming in a pool.
> High law of Singapore said no to that,
> For Indian was black, the water white,
> But poetry put gleaming figures there.[71]

Nicholas Moore made an important contribution to the poetry of the 1940s, but was underrated because often misunderstood, and possibly as well because of his association with the New Apocalypse and with Tambimuttu. "He was a good poet, and because he was my assistant, he has been done in," Tambi believes.[72] But he is a "very individual writer," as Comfort notes, and "a most capable and original poet of enormous fecundity."[73]

Chapter Five
Personalism

Before the publication of the last Apocalyptic anthology, *The Crown and the Sickle* (1944), Treece was already attempting to head another literary movement, Personalism. He and Stefan Schimanski became the editors of four Personalist anthologies entitled *Transformation*. In them they included writers such as Sir Herbert Read, Robert Melville, Robert Herring, Alexander Blok, Anne Ridler, Francis Scarfe, Boris Pasternak, D. S. Savage, Stephen Spender, Cecil Collins, Emmanuel Mounier, Henry Miller, Kenneth Patchen, and Anaïs Nin.

Schimanski was an "expatriate" from Poland who was later killed in an air crash.[1] Herbert Read had introduced him to Treece,[2] and with Treece as poetry editor, Schimanski ran *Kingdom Come*. Wrey Gardiner also knew Schimanski. "Schimanski was a close friend of mine," Gardiner recalls, and "a journalist with considerable interest in contemporary literary movements."[3] With Treece, Schimanski would later edit *A New Romantic Anthology*, published by Gardiner's Grey Walls Press.

According to Treece in a 16 January 1944 letter to Hendry, Personalism or "*Transformation* is a 'popular' approach to Apocalypticism, in a way; a sort of mild indication for a general public of the richness of the spirit, where that spirit functions organically." Treece adds that *Transformation* or Personalism "shows no scuttling, no treachery. It shows only that the Spirit can be approached in a number of ways."[4]

Personalism does add a theory of education, as Baggerly suggests[5] and as Treece and Schimanski's "Towards a Personalist Education" in *Transformation Two* makes clear. Borrowing from the French Personalism of Emmanuel Mounier, Treece and Schimanski write that "Personalism, . . . in the words of Emmanuel Mounier, 'aims at the profound transformation in the realm of pedagogy, with its primacy of

education, i.e., education of the person, over all mere institutions or
erudition, over preparation for crafts or profession, over all class education.' "[6] Furthermore, Treece and Schimanski also provide Personalism with a theological basis. Personalist education should "teach
loyalty and devotion to clearly defined principles—these principles
being the Christian spirit with its basic doctrine of the universal
brotherhood of man." Such a perspective, of course, is not new. Kenneth Rexroth similarly fuses liberal Christianity and anarchism in his
own form of Personalism, as expressed, for example, in *The Phoenix
and the Tortoise* (1944).[7]

The experience of purposelessness or meaninglessness, generated by
the disappearance of absolute values in the modern age, is Paul
Bloomfield's concern in "Letter to a Godson on the Teaching of
Christianity" in *Transformation Two*. Anticipating the revived Wordsworthian transcendentalism in W. T. Stace's *Religion and the Modern
Mind* (1952), Bloomfield fuses nineteenth-century Wordsworthian
transcendentalism or Romanticism and Christianity to argue, as does
Stace, that transcendental values are absolute and that, moreover, the
Personality that is revealed in Nature, as well as by art, is Divine:
". . . what is most spiritual in religion comes from the revelation to
us of a hidden Personality. . . ."[8] The greater theological emphasis
of Personalism is enhanced also by Treece and Schimanski's inclusion
of Lawrence Hyde's "The Realm of the Personal" in *Transformation
Three*. Hyde acknowledges being influenced by Martin Buber's dial-
ogical Jewish Existentialist theology, as expressed in Buber's *I and
Thou* (1937). Such a Buberesque emphasis on dialogue, rather than
Romantic monologue, moves Treece and other poets of the 1940s,
such as Gascoyne,[9] away from the Surrealistic mode. Self-expression
of personality becomes balanced, as in Wordsworth, by the need for
communication.

In *Transformation Two* (1944), Treece and Schimanski included
Read's "Education Through Art," an essay version of his *Education
Through Art*. The sort of aesthetic education which he recommends,
while indebted to Plato's *Republic,* as Read notes, receives "psychological support" from "Gestalt theory":

What they [the Gestaltists] say, in effect, is that there are no facts apart
from the act or process of experiencing them, that the "facts of a case" are
not grasped by enumeration, but must be felt as a coherent pattern.[10]

Read's background as a specialist on contemporary visual art accounts for his appreciation of such central insights of Gestalt psychology. Were he still alive, Read would find compatible Professor Betty Edwards's research into right hemispheral specialization as it relates to drawing. Her work in teaching art students to utilize the right hemisphere suggests that art education may be a means by which students generally may learn how to utilize in other activities outside of art the pattern-recognizing and generating capacities of the brain's right hemisphere. The process of perception which Read describes above in Gestalt language, Edwards describes more persuasively from the perspective of Sperry's work:

In the right-hemisphere mode of information processing, we use intuition and have leaps of insight—moments when "everything seems to fall into place" without figuring things out in logical order. When this occurs, people often spontaneously exclaim, "I've got it" or "Ah, yes, now I see the picture." The classic example of this kind of exclamation is the exultant cry, "Eureka!" (*I have found it!*) attributed to Archimedes.[11]

Read's comments in "Education Through Art" are of this sort. The "factor of feeling in perception" which is "aesthetic" involves a "discrimination" in which a "pattern" is "chosen as being particularly fit or appropriate. It feels right, one feels at once the ease with which this particular pattern is apprehended. . . ." Since the right brain processes information simultaneously, intuitively, and relationally, rather than successively or linearly, Read writes that "the 'facts of a case' are not grasped by enumeration, but must be felt as a coherent pattern."[12] The "felt" quality of such perception may have to do in part with the right brain's more emotional propensities.

In conventional Romantic terminology, the function of education for Treece and Schimanski, following Read's perspective, is to augment the individual's capacity to utilize the imagination through acquainting the individual with imaginative works of visual art, fiction, and poetry, or, as Edwards recommends, through actual artistic creations, as in painting or drawing. Such an education, in the language of Treece and Schimanski in their "Towards a Personalist Education" in *Transformation Two,* would be the "education of the person"[13] rather than the mere enculturation of the person through indoctrination or conditioning. Treece argues that in "History" lessons children should be encouraged to "paint pictures" of historical "scenes," and "if a class is studying the Elizabethan period, let them in Art or Handicraft hours make scale models of Tudor dwelling-houses and furniture, or of the Globe Theater, even of a whole village, . . . let them come to appreciate pattern, form, natural balance and harmony by wandering in the wood. . . ."[14] Arguing in effect for a holistic education of the whole personality, Read concludes his *Transformation Two* essay by writing that "we claim the whole child."[15]

Treece and Schimanski's concept of personality owes much to Read's distinction between character and personality. In *Herbert Read: An Introduction to His Work by Various Hands,* both Treece[16] and Hendry[17] approvingly quote from Read's *Annals of Innocence and Experience* in which Read declares,

A personality . . . is distinguished by immediacy and by what I would call lability, or the capacity to change without the loss of integrity. . . . Character is only attained by limitation.[18]

D. S. Savage, whose own Christian Personalist philosophy is articulated in the earliest issues of *Now,* in *The Personal Principle* (1944) makes essentially the same distinction: "I think that Mr. Read is wrong in identifying the principle of 'life, of creation, of liberation' with romanticism," Savage writes. But he adds that Read "does, however, hit upon an important truth when he identifies what he calls the romantic spirit with the artist and the classic spirit with society, only his terminology is inaccurate. . . ."[19] In *A New Romantic Anthology,* Read writes of "character" as "armor against experience."[20] His conclusion is similar to that of Wilhelm Reich, who invented the concept of character armor as the individual's system of defenses. But it may have been Nietzsche who was influential. In *Joyful Wisdom* Nietzsche distinguishes between static character structure and the personality of the creative intellectual, whom society attempts to repress.

What Read, Savage, Hendry, Treece, Schimanski, and Nietzsche in effect argue against is the overly inhibited personality, who is incapable of autonomous existence and openness to the full range of experience. For "personality," in contrast to "character," Read writes in *Annals of Innocence and Experience,* "the senses are open to every impression which falls upon them. . . ."[21] The idea, at work in Romanticism since Blake, becomes widespread in much Humanistic Psychology after the end of the Second World War. Preoccupied like Read and the Personalists with becoming a fully functioning person, Rogers argues that the therapeutic objective should be to allow "an increasing openness" to experience. "If a person could be fully open" to experience, "every stimulus . . . would be freely relayed through the nervous system without being distorted by any defensive mechanism,"[22] Rogers writes in *On Becoming a Person.*

British Personalists and libertarians in the 1940s anticipate the consciousness-raising, human-potential movements of the 1960s. Again, Read's influence is at work. Treece and Schimanski write,

the expression of the writer's Self and the expression of Society is . . . only a beginning out of which the new type of being, emerging in humanity, will ultimately arise. This is the theme so often treated in Herbert Read's poems, of the gradual emergence of Gods from men; and it is only by way of freedom that men will be able to approach that Godhead.[23]

The language sounds Nietzschean or Blakean, but the intention behind the rhetoric, in any case, has elements in common with Maslow's concept of "self-actualization." Hendry in the first *Transformation* writes, "there *is* no history—except the history of self-realization, which, outside the great of the past, has not yet begun."[24] Similarly, George Woodcock writes that the "primary object" of anarchism "is the realization by the individual of his own nature."[25]

The human motivation toward self-realization Maslow assumes to be innate. It is, in any case, widespread. Apocalypticism, Personalism, and Neo-Romanticism, in this sense, are linked with Wordsworthian preoccupation with the "growth of a poet's mind," Godwin and Shelley's quest for self-perfection, Karen Horney's concept of self-realization, Fromm's emphasis on the individual's "realization of his self, by being himself,"[26] Jung's idea of individuation, Nietzsche's superman, and on the more demonic side, Hitler's "struggle" in *Mein Kampf* and in Europe in the 1940s toward unrestricted expression of the will to power, which inevitably depersonalizes others, and of his private fantasies of universal disaster and cultural rebirth.

Read defines "personalism in art" in the twentieth century generally as a reaction on the part of the artist to the "new freedom" to express in art "his unique personality" which modern psychology engendered after the turn of the century by demonstrating "the validity of individual variations" of personality "type."[27] (Politically, Godwin, Read argues in *Wordsworth,* is a Personalist.[28]) Such conclusions appear to be based largely on Jung's recognition of introverted and extroverted personality types. Moreover, Jung's individuation concept, like Fromm's, stresses the struggle for self-realization as a unique individual, a concept generally compatible with the interest in anarchist, Romantic, and Neo-Romantic theory generally on polymorphism and diversitarian alternatives to Classical and Neo-Classical normative assumptions.

Such antipathies to conformism reappear in Humanistic Psychology. For example, Rogers asks, " 'What am I striving for?' " and answers in "the words of Soren Kierkegaard— 'to be that self which one truly is.' "[29] Hendry may have also had Kierkegaard in mind in writing in *The Crown and the Sickle:* "What are then our real selves? It is man's self as he is daily struggling to be."[30] But the Epigraph for *The White Horseman* provides a more modern model; Treece and Hendry quote from Lawrence's interpretation of the four horsemen of the Apocalypse in his *Apocalypse:*

The rider on the white horse! Who is he, then? . . . He is the royal me, he is my very self and his horse is the whole MANA of a man. He is my very me, my sacred ego, called into a new cycle of action by the Lamb and riding forth to conquest, the conquest of the old self for the birth of a new self.[31]

Personalism, in such a context, represents a reemphasis and clarification of the Personalist orientation of the New Apocalypse which more vaguely emphasizes individual, personal "myth."

Other Personalist themes reflect responses to fascism and echo earlier anarchist concerns, as well as anticipate several of the dominant preoccupations of Western thought in the last half of the twentieth century, from Fromm's *The Fear of Freedom,* published in London in 1941, to Skinner's *Beyond Freedom and Dignity.* Schimanski in "Towards a Personalist Psychology" affirms the "dignity, uniqueness and freedom of man," while arguing that "Man's dignity is rooted in freedom. . . . "[32]

Chapter Six
Libertarian and Neo-Romantic Parallels

The Anarchist Context

The late 1930s and 1940s were primed by international events for an alternative to the Marxist-Freudian liberalism which was identified with the Auden group. The apparent failure of liberalism generally and nationalism to prevent the growing international conflagration and, later, the Stalin-Hitler pact of 1939, were causes of such disillusionment with left-wing solutions to political problems. George Woodcock's *Anarchy of Chaos,* a spirited defense of anarchist theories, was published in 1944, and Alex Comfort's *Art and Social Responsibility,* which included arguments for Romanticism which had anarchist implications, was published in 1946. But earlier, Sir Herbert Read's *Poetry and Anarchism* (1938), *The Philosophy of Anarchism* (1940), and *The Paradox of Anarchism* (1941) had made anarchist theories palatable to intellectuals (partly by creating another image of the anarchist than the popular stereotype of the lean, hunched, Latin male in a dark black cape and ready to throw a bomb in some passing automobile or carriage). Dylan Thomas's art and personality, rather than his ideas, popularized, as well, the image of the artist as an anarchistic rebel. The idea that "the poet is necessarily an anarchist,"[1] Read's conclusion in *Poetry and Anarchism,* had already been ironically and satirically treated by G. K. Chesterton in his conservative *The Man Who Was Thursday.* Such a conclusion is accepted also by Woodcock and implied by Comfort in *Art and Social Responsibility,* which is dedicated to Read.

Surrealism also may have prepared the way for a revival of anarchism through its frontal assault on establishment values. But the 1940s also saw a revival of interest in Peter Kropotkin's anarchist the-

ories: in particular, his research into the principle of species solidarity
or "mutual aid" (as presented in *Mutual Aid,* 1902). Comfort, Woodcock, and the poet and novelist Alfred Marnau, an "anarcho-mon-
archist,"[2] all base their social philosophy on Kropotkin's theory of
"mutual aid."

The anarchist tendencies of the 1940s poets are evident in writers,
such as Kenneth Patchen, Wrey Gardiner, Paul Goodman, D. S. Savage, and George Woodcock, whose works appear in *New Road: New
Directions in Art and Letters,* edited by Bayliss and Comfort and later
by Marnau, and Comfort's *Poetry Folios.* In an essay on "Ezra Pound's
Guilt" in *Poetry Folios* (London, 1946), Patchen declares: "Let this be
made clear. There is no man in authority anywhere who is not guilty.
All their authority is evil—founded on hatred and darkness, not on
love; designed to destroy—not to save."[3] In "Eve of St. Agony or the
Middle-class Was Sitting on Its Fat," Patchen, the verbal and ideo-
logical exhibitionist, tells of going "in for strip-teasing before/Save
Democracy/Clubs," and in "The Hangman's Great Hands" pro-
claims: *"Those smug saints, whether of church or Stalin,/Can get off the
back of my people, and stay off."* Less rhetorically, Savage in *The Personal
Principle: Studies in Modern Poetry* (1944) argues that the modern artist
"can no longer rely on any external authority—indeed, there *is* no
external authority."[4]

William Morris in his quasi-anarchist romance *News from Nowhere*
expresses the conventional libertarian objection to government: it exists for the "protection of the rich from the poor, the strong from the
weak."[5] He does not exclude democractic government from such criticism. Similarly, J. F. Hendry, finding a spokesman in the fourteenth
century in "John Ball, Priest, to the Nation (1382)," indirectly alludes to his own disillusionment with government and democracy's
ineffectuality in the histrionic 1930s and 1940s, in which pageantry,
as that of the Nuremberg rallies, masks insidious intent:

> Now, on behalf of my generation,
> I accept with thanks from the Nation
> Anger, disillusion and regret
> That there is no real improvement yet.
> Anger at our melodramatic time
> And all the pomp and circumstance of crime
> Disillusion at the circus
> In the Parliamentary House.[6]

In a sense, Neo-Romanticism, like Romanticism, represents a reaction to the political theories of more Classically directed poets, with MacNeice and Auden replacing Johnson and Pope. But both the Auden group and the Neo-Romantics, such as Read, Treece, Hendry, Comfort, Stanford, and Gardiner, are similar in their rejection of capitalism. To some extent the antipathy of such Neo-Romantics to capitalism, as well as that of Auden, Day Lewis, and Spender, represents an extension of conventional religious and literary judgments upon Western materialism. In *The White Horseman,* Hendry writes of "our meaningless search for material wealth"[7] and in "John Ball, Priest, to the Nation (1382)" indirectly attacks contemporary materialism. But he attacks also contemporary Capitalist exploitation of the workers through a system of usury, Pound's concern, and capitalism's dehumanizing tendency to evaluate human worth from the perspective of acquired wealth:

> You have made the King a Moneylender:
> The Nation's means and meaning slender.
> Money is minted by your servitude.
> Your standard of value is fear. Am I rude?
> However you shout and bully and rage
> I will not be paid in such a wage. . . .
>
> Ambition's chained to arithmetic and gold. . . .

Such Neo-Romantic criticism of capitalism overlaps that of Marx, who criticized large-scale capitalism for alienating the worker from the product of his labors. In *How I See Apocalypse,* Treece defends anarchism by arguing that under anarchism the worker "will do a good job because he will be using his production himself. . . . " Like earlier anarchists attracted to the more simple economic system of bartering, Treece views money, the invention which helps make capitalism possible, as an impersonalizing and dehumanizing agent: under anarchism, the worker "will wish to barter them [his 'productions'] with another local 'collective,' in return for goods which he does not create."[8]

Decentralized communal collectives rather than centralized communism is Treece's objective. In *How I See Apocalypse,* he argues for "small, local 'collectives,' "[9] and later with Stefan Schimanski in *Transformation* (volume one) argues for "the smallest of co-operative collectives where each member is acknowledged as the other's equal. . . . "[10] Similarly, Woodcock argues in *New Life to the Land* (1942) for decentralized, equalitarian "co-operatives."[11] With Savage, Woodcock attempted to put such idealism into practice: "He and I . . . were very close for a period," Woodcock recalls, "when we tried to set up an intentional community on pacifist principles in Cambridgeshire. . . . "[12] The desire for decentralization is deeply engrained in the anarchist perspective. Exploiting the popular notion of the pastoral Golden Age, Godwin in *Imogen* represents a decentralized community and intimates a future in which for mankind generally the world of Imogen will be recaptured. William Morris's quasi-anarchist utopia in *News from Nowhere* is similarly decentralized, and much of the blight of noise and smoke pollution which affected London gone with centralization: Walthamstow and Woodford have become a "pretty place," one of Morris's characters explains, " 'now that the trees have had time to grow again since the great clearing of houses in 1955.' "[13] Centralization is a primary cause of the growth toward tyranny in Olivero's worldly utopia in Part Two of *The Green Child*, and in Read's *Aristotle's Mother*, Aristotle's "reason tells him that the happiest men live in the smallest communities. . . . "[14]

The function of law in controlling behavior in centralized society in which anonymity isolates the individual from primary-group controls is accepted by most sociologists. In effect, Treece in *How I See Apocalypse* is arguing for prioritizing primary groups, which largely determine moral behavior and in which individuals relate to each other with intimacy, trust, and as complete human beings: "Keep the group small enough for intimacy among its units," Treece advises in *How I See Apocalypse*, "so that men do not lose the sense of neighbourly decency. . . . "[15] And later he adds, "In the political condition I am trying to outline, a man's first duty is to the farm or workshop which he is sharing with the other men of his street or village."[16]

Such an emphasis on economic "sharing" also extends back to Godwin and is present as well in Morris's *News from Nowhere*, in which everyone shares gladly and freely, and, as a consequence, there are no poor people. Poets influenced by Marxism have a similar vision of the just society. Spender in "Not Palaces, an Era's Crown," envisions a society in which "No one/Shall hunger: Man shall spend equally."

But anarchist notions of equality involve equalizing both wealth and authority, as in Godwin's pastoral utopia in *Imogen:* "Of all the shepherds of the valley, there is not one that claims dominion and command over another."[17] Shelley in *Prometheus Unbound* envisions the regaining of the lost egalitarian paradise:

> And behold, thrones were kingless, and men walked
> One with the other even as spirits do,
> None fawned. . . .
>
> The loathsome mask has fallen, the man remains
> Sceptreless, free, uncircumscribed, but man
> Equal, unclassed, tribeless, and nationless,
> Exempt from awe, worship, degree, the king
> Over himself. . . .

To the extent that 1930s writers like Auden and Spender accept the Marxist vision of a final anarchist utopia, their objectives are, again, essentially the same as those of Treece, Woodcock, Read, Gardiner, Hendry, and other anarchists. For Marxists, however, anarchist communism will emerge only after the so-called dictatorship of the proletariat and the withering away of the state. Spender in "Not Palaces, an Era's Crown," writes: "Man shall spend equally./Our goal which we compel: Man shall be man." The essential difference between Spender and the anarchist writers of the 1940s in this respect is that, like earlier anarchists, they advocate a form of communism which is not compelled, or externally imposed, by authoritarian means, but which develops from unrepressed in-built principles, like those producing the "golden lemon" in Read's "A Song for the Spanish Anarchists":

> The golden lemon is not made
>   but grows on a green tree:
> A strong man and his crystal eyes
>   is a man born freed.
>
> The oxen pass under the yoke
>   and the blind are led at will:
> But a man born free has a path of his own
>   and a house on the hill.

> And men are men who till the land
> and women are women who weave:
> Fifty men own the lemon grove
> and no man is a slave.

"With Tree as Unity"

The tree is a primary metaphor for anarchism, as well as Romanticism, as Chesterton satirically suggests in *The Man Who Was Thursday*. Gregory, the presumed anarchist poet, addresses Syme, the poet of repectability, law, and order. Gregory with his stick strikes a lamp-post and then a tree:

"About *this* and *this*," he cried; about order and anarchy. There is your precious order, that lean, iron lamp, ugly and barren; and there is anarchy, rich, living, reproducing itself—there is anarchy, splendid in green and gold.[18]

In "With Tree as Unity" in *How I See Apocalypse,* Treece, non-satirically assuming the anarchoromantic perspective of Read, argues that "Man's growth and education are like the processes of a tree. . . . " He adds that the tree obeys "no laws but those of the earth and air, the fundamental edicts of Nature."[19]

Pedagogically, Treece's tree metaphor, like Read's "golden lemon" metaphor, implies that educators should allow in-built or biologically preprogrammed propensities to work with little interference, a conclusion which is shared by Paul Goodman and other anarchists in the 1940s, as well as by earlier Rousseauian liberals, and to some extent by nineteenth-century Romantics generally. Blake in "Proverbs of Hell" informs his readers: "The apple tree never asks the beech how he shall grow. . . . " In "Selections From a Poem in Progress," Treece implies much the same meaning: "There is a tree within a spinning seed. . . . "

The horticultural analogy, however, allows interference with the environment, metaphorically the soil, in which the individual or plant develops. Hendry in *Fernie Brae: a Scottish Childhood* (1949) writes of "a wider environment necessary if life were to expand like a flower. . . . "[20] Such conclusions are similar to those of Read, who in *Education Through Art* approvingly quotes Trigant Burrow: " 'One may let a child grow up, naturally, as a plant, tending only the soil about its roots. . . . ' "[21] A more modern variant is Carl Rogers's libertarian "non-directive" therapy.

Belief in the inherent goodness and purposefulness of the human species links some Neo-Romantics, such as Read and Treece, with contemporary personality theorists such as Rogers and Maslow. Moreover, the assumption that human nature is inherently good extends to the philosophy of style: e.g., Wordsworth's preference for the language of ordinary, uncultivated persons and the Neo-Romantics' Surrealistic tendency seemingly to bypass to a large extent the reservoir of culture, so evident in Eliot's poetry, in favor of the personal reservoir of the untutored, uncivilized unconscious. Such views seem Rousseauian. But Neo-Romantics produce Freudian monsters from the depths of the unconscious as well as innate tendencies toward sociability; and Read, Comfort, and Gardiner's Neo-Romanticism is based on the pessimistic assumption that the tendency of the human species to abuse power and behave pathologically in groups is, like Adamic depravity, innate.

Neo-Romanticism is more process oriented than is either Eliot's Neo-Classicism or the *New Lines* Movement of the 1950s. In this sense also Neo-Romantics anticipate the development of Humanistic Psychology after the war. The ideal emphasis of a just society, according to Rogers, "would be upon man as a process of becoming. . . . "[22] Hulme argued that human nature is "absolutely constant" and that the species in evolution, following De Vrie's mutation theory rather than Darwin's, are also "absolutely fixed."[23] The ideal line of development, from such a perspective, is largely to attain the perfection of the type, or, after Plato, the ideal prototype.

In contrast, Neo-Romanticism repeats the revolt of earlier anarchism and Romanticism against legal and Classical absolutes. As in Rogers's nondirective therapy, the growth of personality is "away from pleasing others," "from oughts," and "from meeting expectations," and toward autonomy, "self-direction," and "trust of self."[24]

Aesthetically, the Surrealistic mode, whether in Treece, Hendry, or Gascoyne, like stream-of-consciousness fiction, emphasizes process rather than product, in conventional literary terminology. Treece's "tree" and Read's "stream" in *The Green Child* are process symbols.

Some of the titles of Treece's poetry also suggest process mentality, such as *Toward a Personal Armageddon* and "The Never-Ending Rosary."

The traditional anarchist and Romantic distinction between the organic and mechanic is at work in the poetry of the 1940s. But for anarchist poets, such as Woodcock and Read, unlike organicists such as Carlyle, mechanization is fundamentally the product of power orientation in society. Godwin was concerned about authoritarian institutions reducing "the exertions of a human being to the level of a piece of mechanism . . . alleviated by no genuine passion."[25] Shelley in *Queen Mab* writes that the

> . . . virtuous soul commands not, nor obeys.
> Power, like a desolating pestilence,
> Pollutes what'er it touches; and obedience
> Bane of all genius, virtue, freedom, truth,
> Makes slaves of men, and of the human frame
> A mechanized automation.

"The Mass of men serve the state," Thoreau declared, " . . . not as men mainly, but as machines, with their bodies."[26] Later anarchists, such as Bakunin, Tolstoy, Kropotkin, and Read, adopt essentially the same perspective. Depersonalization, the experience of being merely a cog in the machine of modern government or bureaucracy, is involved, as in D. S. Savage's "Factory," in which are described "the mechanic minds of unquestioning men,/their smooth-limbed bodies, and the soft voice of death."

Mechanization implies a loss of spontaneity. Simply stated, the experience of mechanization in nineteenth- and twentieth-century literature is often the consequence of punishment or the threat of punishment. Read's argument that the anarchist is the man who dares in adulthood "to resist the authority of the father"[27] may be interpreted from such a perspective: it is the conscience or superego, the product of the internalization of the judgments of the father or father surrogates, which represses or inhibits natural or organic tendencies and leaves mechanical or compulsive patterns of behavior.

Where the argument for spontaneity is extended to art, as in Wordsworth or the Apocalyptics' interest in taming the spontaneous muse of Surrealism, Neo-Classical poets, who seem to follow or advocate externally imposed aesthetic norms, appear mechanical. In a letter of 8 September 1941 thanking Comfort for a favorable review of *The White Horseman,* Treece most probably has Auden, Day Lewis, and MacNeice in mind: " . . . I hope that it [*The White Horseman*] will have some effect on the course of poetry; an antidote to the Mechanists has been needed for years."[28]

You Can Go Home Again

An alternative in Neo-Romanticism to being mechanized or overly conditioned by society is shedding one's conditioning, like Siloën in *The Green Child* sheds her restrictive clothes in her underground world, and becoming once more like a preconditioned child. Regaining a childlike sense of innocence, spontaneity, awe, and ecstasy, as in more recent Maslowian humanistic psychology, is the objective of much nineteenth-century Romantic and twentieth-century Neo-Romantic art, from Blake to Thomas, Read, Patchen, and Treece. Moreover, at work in Neo-Romanticism also is a widespread dissatisfaction—evident as well in Jung—with the alienation of the human species from nature and the child's alienation from his environment through the development of consciousness and a sense of self-identity. Regaining childhood bliss for some Neo-Romantics involves regaining a sense of oneness with the natural environment before the "fall" from Eden's "grace," in Thomas's language, into subject-object awareness of separation.

Dominated by the superego and time and conceptually topheavy, Read's Olivero in *The Green Child* is impelled to return in memory as well as in fact to England, the country of his childhood. The green child he seeks (probably green because Read, like Thomas, finds green symbolic of childhood and man's organic ties with nature) represents in part the repressed and lost child in Olivero. Rediscovering Siloën, in this context, involves for Olivero rediscovering the child locked within. Descent into the pool to the underground world suggests baptism, as Woodcock suggests, or symbolic death, through submersion in water.[29] It suggests as well that Neo-Romantic regression pushed far enough involves rebirth into a different mode of existence.

Neo-Romantic preoccupation with childhood seems most directly indebted to Thomas, Barker, and Wordsworth, rather than to Read.

But Hendry's autobiographical *Fernie Brae* is reminiscent of Read's *The Green Child,* poetry, autobiographical works, such as *Annals of Innocence and Experience* (1940), and theories of education and art (as well as Dickens's depiction of repressive education in *Hard Times*):

> School itself was the greatest shock to pristine wholeness. This was being "educated," learning you were a hopeless fumbling fool at sewing patterns of strips and scraps of coloured paper, that you would never be anything else; that the scissors and blue and weaving and intricacy of thought and shape and loopholes in design were all forever beyond you, so no use trying. . . .
>
> Now at school he had suddenly learned that he must not dream or feel or imagine anything, but think, fit into shape, make coloured patterns and cardboard models from rigid enervating lines.[30]

Like Read's *The Green Child,* Treece's "Oh Child" presents the archetypal child as an agent of redemption and renewal. But more in the Romantic tradition is Treece's "Poem" beginning "After a little while" in *The New Apocalypse.* Treece recalls the seemingly unavoidable condition of childhood in which low self-esteem, partly caused by dependency, helps to generate high-dominance fantasies:

> I was the lad caught thunder in his cap,
> And taught the hawk to carve his name on clouds, . . .
>
> . . . he whose needs
> Were those alone that motivate the birds
> To ride wild winds or rest content in woods.

Similar high-dominance fantasies are at work in Comfort's "First Elegy" and Thomas's "Fern Hill": " . . . honored among wagons I was prince of the apple towns. . . . / . . . the calves/Sang to my horn . . . "; Treece's child who teaches the hawk; Comfort's child who has dominion over his childhood "friends" and "playmates" (animals); and Thomas's child who is lord of his apple-town kingdom (Fern Hill) are variations of the same theme. Children are fond of animals partly because they can imaginatively or literally establish dominance over them. Eden is the implied metaphor in the poems of Treece and Comfort and the explicit metaphor in "Fern Hill": the child is newly created Adam being given by God dominion over all the "fowl of the air" and the beasts of the field (Genesis 1:28).

Freudian, Jungian, and Neo-Romantic approaches to experience allow emotionally charged states of consciousness in which the stages of life—childhood, adulthood, and sometimes old age—are experienced simultaneously. Read presents the phenomenon in *The Green Child* allegorically. Treece in "Remembering Last Year" finds and defines himself: "Urchin and ancient, stand I in my grief," recalling Thomas's "Poem in October," which similarly depicts the urchin doppelgänger, the equivalent of Read's green child: "his tears burned my cheeks and his heart moved in mine," Thomas laments. Also tearful, Woodcock in "Buntingsdale" envisions, like Treece, the urchin and ancient, what he was and is to be:

> There stand a boy and an old man beside me,
> And I am both, yet am between and neither.
> The boy has wasted within me, yet is unmourned,
> Within me the old man grows, yet is unborn. . . .

But unlike Thomas, Woodcock returns to childhood in order to understand it well enough to become emotionally detached from it: hence, what appears to be an ironic reference to Thomas's "I See the Boys of Summer." Whereas Thomas sees the boys of summer "in their ruin," Woodcock leaves the boy "to weep on his own ruin": i.e., refuses to be trapped by obsessional anger or despair over the loss of childhood. The Wordsworthian perspective which is at the base of both poems is that the human condition is distinguished from that of lower forms of life inasmuch as human consciousness involves grief over the loss of childhood: " . . . while the young lambs bound / . . . To me alone there came a thought of grief" ("Ode: Intimations of Immortality"). Poems recording child-to-adulthood changes do not of course necessarily emphasize loss, deprivation, or the superiority of childhood; Pound's "The River-Merchant's Wife: A Letter" depicts stages in the maturation process and their implication to present consciousness. What has "departed" in Pound's poem is the husband-lover, not the visionary splendor and the dream. Wordsworth famously finds compensation and consolation in the thought that although "nothing can bring back the hour/Of splendour in the grass, of glory in the flower," we may "grieve not," finding, rather, "strength in what remains behind. . . . "[31] The consolation of Woodcock's poem is somewhat analogous, although it also recalls Thomas Wolfe's *You Can't Go Home Again* (1940). Like Wolfe's Monk and Read's Olivero, Woodcock, or his persona, returns to the geographical scenes of his childhood.

But the environment has altered, not because partly modernized (as in Wolfe and Read), but because the mind and body have enlarged (making the child's world seem shrunken). It is more significantly diminished, however, because, as in Treece's "Y Ddraig Goch," it is no longer haunted by the grandiose products of the child's fantasy and imagination:

> Beyond the green mill, the path where a loon was caught,
> The wall a vixen leaped and summer house of experiments
> In physiology and verse confront me on this hill—
> The same, yet shrunken in a world shaped like the past.
>
> The view is mean. The tall panorama of boyhood
> Has died in its earth and trees. Standing, I remember—
> Deliberately—our grandiose names of ditches.
> The path is Appian. The wall of China. The dull summer
>   house Arthurian Camelot.

Neo-Romantic literature also treats the possibility of negative regression. Romanticism and Read's Neo-Romanticism tend to favor primitives and peasants, in art representing for some Romantics and Neo-Romantics a positive cultural regression to the childhood of the human species. But docility, obedience, and dependency are not a desirable objective. Moreover, in post-Freudian Neo-Romantic art repressed infantile lust may charge regressive fantasies with both terror and Oedipal desire or lead to sublimation through art, as in Barker's "True Confessions": "Track any poet to a beginning/And in a dark room you discover/A little boy intent on sinning/With an etymological lover."

But in general Neo-Romanticism, influenced by Freud's belief that repressed childhood memories need to be rediscovered, is based on an assumption that the remembrance of things past is a means of achieving psychic wholeness.

The Holy Grail: Wholeness

What the Neo-Romantics and related libertarian poets of the 1940s felt to be missing in the poetry of the Auden group was partly a quality of psychological or spiritual wholeness: as in Barker's "Resolution and Dependence," Neo-Romantics, intent on "finding an equation" or meaning to existence, often come to conclude that "The equation is the interdependence of parts." Nicholas Moore, disliking the tenets of Apocalypticism and feeling alienated from Neo-Romanticism, nevertheless related to Apocalypticism's emphasis on wholeness: "The part of the Apocalyptic movement that appealed to me . . . was the idea of 'completeness' of the 'whole man,' of the poet alive in all his senses and capable of using them to proper effect." Fraser, also growing alienated, and Tom Scott, whose poetry is included in *The White Horseman,* were similarly interested in obtaining psychological integration or wholeness. D. S. Savage begins his *The Personal Principle* by observing that if its "theme" "could be expressed in one word, that word would be Wholeness or Integrity."[32]

The completeness sought generally involved the sort of reconciliation of the claims of the imagination and the reason that was intended in nineteenth-century Romanticism. Explaining the symbolism of the title of *The Crown and the Sickle,* the third Apocalyptic anthology, Treece writes in his "Preface":

The crown is glory, victory, the imagination; the sickle is the surgical reason. The two together are symbols of man's completeness, and it is totality of experience which this collection attempts to portray.

Treece's symbols are the modern equivalents of Wordsworth's stone and shell in his apocalyptic dream vision in Book V of *The Prelude.* The stone which he receives from the Arab seer is " 'Euclid's Elements' " and symbolizes the preferred mode of reasoning in eighteenth-century Neo-Classicism: abstract, sometimes geometric conceptualization. But the shell, like Treece's crown, is paramount or symbolizes " 'something of more worth' ":[33] the imagination in general and perhaps as well what Wordsworth understood to be the imagination in its apocalyptic mode. Holding the shell to his ear, the dreaming Wordsworth hears a "loud prophetic blast of harmony;/An

Ode, in passion uttered, which foretold/Destruction to the children of the earth/By deluge, now at hand."[34]

From a more recent and biological perspective, Romanticism and Neo-Romanticism seem in part expressions of functional lateralization. R. W. Sperry, basing his conclusions on the radical surgery on epileptics of his colleague Philip Vogel, has noted that the brain's left hemisphere is the locus for "calculation" and the brain's "main language center": the right hemisphere is responsible for "spacial construction" and "nonverbal ideation."[35] Professors Carl Sagan and Betty Edwards, basing their conclusions on the work of Sperry and Vogel, argue that the brain's left hemisphere, which controls the right side of the body, dominates civilization: " 'Right' is associated with legality, correct behavior, high moral principles,"[36] etc. If so, Neo-Romanticism, as well as nineteenth-century Romanticism, may represent in part an artistic revolt in favor of a more complete realization of the abilities of the repressed, neglected right hemisphere, which works symbolically, visually (through images, that is), holistically, metaphorically, emotionally, and analogically, as compared to the dominant left hemisphere, which works abstractly, verbally, linearly, literally, and logically.

Hemispheral specialization may also be one cause, probably small, of the atmosphere of gloom and doom in Romanticism and Neo-Romanticism. Sagan cites "recent experiments by Stuart Dimond," of the University College, Cardiff in Wales, which show "a remarkable tendency for the right hemisphere to view the world as more unpleasant, hostile, and even disgusting than the left hemisphere."[37] In *The Contrary Experience,* Read, to avoid despair, turns to reason, which Read, like Treece, symbolizes as a sickle:

Through all the mutations of these years I have relied on a weapon which I found in my hand as soon as I was compelled to abandon my innocent vision and fight against the despairs of experience. This weapon is . . . like the sickle. . . . Such a weapon is reason, which alone can slay despair. . . .[38]

Although Sperry, Vogel, and later researchers have demonstrated that both hemispheres may function in either complete or relative isolation from each other, it is more a matter of relative emphasis in poetry than of discreet hemispheral function. Eighteenth- and Auden-generation Neo-Classical poetry is relatively verbal, logical, and abstract, but, like painting and sculpture, is also holistically structured. On the other hand, even the illogical poems of Thomas and Gascoyne are verbal and scanned linearly as well as perceived as a gestalt.

Alex Comfort

"In better times," Treece writes to Alex Comfort on 22 October 1941, "I would like to represent you in a further Apocalyptic Anthology." Comfort's poetry and "The Martyrdom of the House," an antiwar short story, are in fact included in the last Apocalyptic anthology, *The Crown and the Sickle.* Concerning "The Martyrdom of the House," Treece wrote to Comfort on 27 August 1942: "It is shocking. I consider it to be the sort of thing I want, apocalyptic in a real, violent sense."

The most theoretically developed manifesto of Neo-Romanticism is probably Comfort's *Art and Social Responsibility* (1946). Comfort's "An Exposition of Irresponsibility," which Treece and Schimanski include in *A New Romantic Anthology,* represents an earlier version. Comfort is a more original anarchist theorist than Treece, yet his conclusions also take into account a wider range of libertarian theorists, such as Kropotkin, Godwin, Proudhon, and Fromm. The influence of Kropotkin on Treece, by contrast, essentially comes indirectly through Read, who is his elegiac "The Death of Kropotkin" finds Kropotkin a "prophet" and "dear comrade and pioneer" whom "many will follow."

Comfort's Neo-Romanticism differs from Treece's Apocalypticism and Personalism in placing greater emphasis on science and the external environment. In conventional literary terminology, Comfort's Neo-Romanticism incorporates Classical and Neo-Classical respect for lucidity, rationality, analysis, and inquisitiveness about the physical and social environment with Romantic respect for intuition, imagination, holism and synthesis, and inwardness. In Sperry's language, Comfort's Neo-Romanticism represents a more even balance between left and right hemispheral functions.

It also revives more than does Apocalypticism and Personalism the emphasis in earlier forms of anarchism and Romanticism on nonrepressive sexuality. In this sense it has something in common with the American anarchism in the 1940s and 1950s of Paul Goodman, who seems also to have been influenced by Read. Comfort's Neo-Romanticism, however, has more in common with Camus's art and philosophy of permanent rebellion as a necessary alternative to political revolutions. In conventional literary terminology, Comfort's Neo-Romantic ideology may be said to represent the application of the process-product distinction of traditional Romanticism to political behavior: it advocates a process of growing but never-ending rebellion rather than a revolutionary product—the creation, that is, of another form of society and government.

Mythologically, such Neo-Romantic speculations express the sense of endless rebellion against authority at work in Camus's *The Myth of Sisyphus,* while reaffirming that element of anarchism which Godwin, Read, and Shelley emphasize: the combination of victimization and defiance or rebelliousness against all irrational patterns of authority to be found in Godwin's Imogen and Caleb Williams, Read's Green Child, and Shelley's Prometheus.

The Visionary Mode

Treece's excited outbursts of utopian fantasizing in *How I See Apocalypse* represent a significantly less disillusioned perspective on the possibilities for social change:

Yet what I am asking for, and this may be nothing more than a young man's dream has ever been, is not primarily a revised economic system, the destruction of caste and privilege, . . . the abolition of dividends. . . . It is A CHANGE OF HEART. I am asking that for once since the dawn of human life on this earth men might see sense . . . allow themselves to act and believe according to the spark of decency and rightness that *must* be a human possession if being is to have any point at all save that of manuring the soil.

If for one second on any day all men walking about on the surface of the earth could feel and recognize the nature and existence of this spark, I think Heaven would have come.[39]

Allowing for poetic license, Treece's conclusions also represent a secular version of the Christian notion of bringing about the Kingdom of God in society through personal conversion. Spender's concern with "a change of heart" in *The Destructive Element*[40] and Auden's with "a change of heart" in "Petition" may have influenced Treece's formulation. Such a formulation indirectly announces the political rebel's willingness to tolerate nonviolent evolutionary development toward ideal social and political goals.

Treece had perhaps first used his change-of-heart formula in a 3 September 1941 letter to Comfort in which Treece writes of *"a change of heart*—not a communist or any other change of heart, but the mere desire and ability to recognize at some time the Good and to cast away the Bad." Treece adds,

> But that knowledge, that belief and that desire to be sane and reasonable is sadly lacking, even among the philosophers. For instance, there goes Middleton-Murray—a man whose criticism I have always admired in the past—unable to understand Read's anarchism.

Such an emphasis on social change through personal redemption is ubiquitous in anarchist thought and is usually linked with utopian implications, as in Godwin's *Imogen* and Shelley's *Prometheus Unbound*. Where pessimism or realism modify utopian expectations, the poet-prophet may come to conclude that the Kingdom of God is within. But if utopian expectations are not demythologized, as it were, but unrealizable in the poet's lifetime, the apocalyptic poet may find the blissful and fusional qualities of romantic love a foretaste of the bliss and harmony of paradise.

George Woodcock. Woodcock's "Waterloo Bridge" provides an example and also presents another consolation: that found in identification with the faithful dead who were also denied, like Moses, entrance to the promised land:

> These are the praised, remembered in verse and stone,
> Multiplied in the actions of the living,
> These are the great whose earthly dead has grown
> In an existence greater than their death.
> Above the striving and above the raving
> They soar, as vast as gods, as light as breath.
> I know they did not fail, they did not die
> As we who live our dying blasphemy.
>
> I know no world infected their desires
> Or sapped their deeds. . . .

> . . . The lantern brain
> Lit them a way I see that we must run
> If we, my love, would live beyond the hand
> That coils our life into a twist of pain.
> Our selves within our hearts we must create,
> Like seeds in flower and flowers involvulate. . . .
>
> . . . We must forget our fear,
> Ignore the deadly world and make, my love,
> Our music of the spiritual ear.
> Breathing, as gods, our mountain air of truth
> We may escape the daily hour of death.

A possible model for Woodcock's "Waterloo Bridge" is Shelley's *The Revolt of Islam*. Shelley's Cythna, like Woodcock or his persona, refers to those who are "great" while addressing her "love"; and her view of the lover's paradise within as a compensation for personal death and foretaste of a harmonious utopia is much the same:

> O dearest love! we shall be dead and cold
> Before this morn may on the world arise;
> Wouldst thou the glory of its dawn behold?
> Alas! gaze not on me, but turn thine eyes
> On thine own heart—it is a paradise
> Which everlasting Spring has made its own,
> And while drear Winter fills the naked skies,
> Sweet streams of sunny thought, and flowers flesh-blown,
> Are there, and weeve their sounds and odours into one.
>
> In their own hearts the earnest of the hope
> Which made them great, the good will ever find. . . .[41]

Although not written by a member of Treece and Hendry's Apocalpytic group, "Waterloo Bridge" is as apocalyptic in character, if not more so, than Treece and Hendry's visionary poems.

Like Treece in "To the Edge and Back," Watkins in "The Broken Sea," and Moore at the conclusion of "The River in the Sun," Woodcock adopts the stance of the poet as seer. "I see the plane caught in the crossed hands of light," Woodcock writes, and, later, in imagery that seems momentarily to transform Woodcock's faithful dead into

St. John's horsemen of the Apocalypse, writes: "I see the statues rising from their rests, / The famous riding again above the city / That dies beneath their iron galaxy." (A similar intimation of St. John's apocalyptic horsemen occurs in Bayliss's Neo-Romantic "Apocalypse and Resurrection," influenced by the New Apocalypse: "I have seen the white horsemen riding to hell / with their legions fast as light, fierce and inevitable . . .").

Such apocalyptic poems are not uniformly optimistic. "Waterloo Bridge" is darker in tone than *The Revolt of Islam*. Darker still is Julian Symon's Trotskyan "Mr. Symons at Richmond, Mr. Pope at Twickenham." Thinking of Pope, the "malicious / Dwarf," who represents the sort of hypocrisy and lack of "self-knowledge" that Symons finds at work in the present age, Symons concludes:

> *My sorrow is every man's, who requires so little*
> *More than immediate happiness, immediate love.*
> *Must I look at injustice? Is any other*
> *World real?*

Woodcock's "Sunday on Hampstead Heath," by contrast, captures much of the optimism of Shelley's early Godwinian period. With friends, apparently anarchists talking of imprisonment, the poet daydreams of a world renewed:

> Here on the hilltop my friends and I sit down.
> They talk of prisons; the conversation falls
> And I say: "One evening we must drink at Spaniards."
> I do not know what they are thinking as their heels
> Kick out the turf and their gaze creeps over the scene,
> Peering through the smoke for the customary landmarks.
>
> But, going away in my mind from their shut faces,
> Away from the quiet hilltop and the leisurely men
> Digging in their new gardens below in the little valley,
> I enter the forest of rooftops; under the grimy stone
> I walk among the pipedreams of men in braces
> Reading in Sunday newspapers the end of faith and folly.
>
> And in the broken slums see the benign lay down
> Their empty, useless loves, and the stunted creep

Ungainly and ugly, towards a world more great
Than the moneyed hopes of masters can ever shape.
In the dead, grey streets I hear the women complain
And their voice is a spark to burn the myth of the state.
And here where my friends talk and the green leaves spurt
Quietly from waterlogged earth, and the dry leaves bud,
I see a world may rise as golden as Blake
Knew in his winged dreams, and the leaves of good
Burst out on branches dead from winter's hurt.
Then the lame may rise and the silent voices speak.

Woodcock's reference to burning "the myth of the state" established his anarchist perspective. But in much the same way that visions of apocalyptic catastrophe expressed the 1930s fear of the approaching end of civilization, Woodcock's vision of Blake's world renewed in "Sunday on Hampstead Heath" expressed a widespread hope among writers, the "feeling," as Spender recalls, "that after the war a better world must come into existence: an England like Blake's Jerusalem."[42]

"Sunday on Hampstead Heath" is a reminder that the concept of apocalypse involves more than end-of-the-world fantasies and feelings of impending doom. The apocalyptic imagination creates also visions of restoration. Out of the holocaust of Armageddon will arise, Phoenix-like, a new Eden: a public and communal Eden to match the private Eden of childhood regained in Romantic and Neo-Romantic poetry.

Biologically, the human species may be preprogrammed, as Sagan suggests, nostalgically to pine after, and in fleeting images imagine, the Eden or Golden Age of the species. In any case, such paradisiacal fantasies seem often to imply an analogous integration with the environment to that which is apparently an objective in Romantic regressive flights to childhood's bliss. Metaphors of natural renewal work from the opposite direction to suggest Nature becoming more integrated with human needs and aspirations.

But in "Sunday on Hampstead Heath" such metaphors express as well the traditional anarchist view of history, which is similar to that expressed by Christian mythology: Eden, expulsion into a period of conflict with coercive society, and Paradise regained. Woodcock's images of seasonal renewal—"leaves of Good / Burst out on branches dead from winter's hurt"—echo those of Shelley's famous West-Wind ode or *Hellas,* in which the "world's great age begins anew" as the "earth doth like a snake renew / Her winter weeds outworn. . . ."

Woodcock is also capable of soberly and realistically expressing the sense of despair and alienation experienced by pacifist anarchists during the war. His "Poem from London, 1941" suggests that the war, producing European refugees, had universalized the anarchist experience: "kissed onward by the pistol, we are all exile, / Expatriate, wandering in the illusive streets / Of faked identify."

But apocalyptic visions, less limited by the reality principle, do not usually work in half-measure. Shelley's vision of the world beginning "anew" is typical, as is Comfort's vision in "None But My Foe to Be My Guide": "Though they have taken so much, we still remain / . . . and in the end we are makers of new things."

Watkins, Thomas, and Barker. Vernon Watkins, who is included in Gardiner's *A New Romantic Anthology,* seems, as Gardiner notes, "definitely romantic." Watkins has been identified by literary historians with the Apocalyptic Movement largely because he is included in *The White Horseman.* But Watkins, like Thomas, never endorsed the Apocalyptic Movement, disassociated himself from it, and became angry at Treece, in particular, for including his poetry in *The White Horseman.* Treece's understanding of the matter is suggested by his 15 January 1942 letter to Comfort: "I resent the comment, copy from Watkins, that he knew nothing of *The White Horseman* until it arrived at his house. He was asked to contribute and sent stuff. That's just a bit of eyewash."

It was Watkins's "The Mummy" and "Mana" which Read apparently suggested to Hendry for *The White Horseman,* as indicated in one of Hendry's letters to Treece (6 November 1940). "The Mummy," which in its subject matter recalls Thomas's more jocular "Should Lanterns Shine," is hypnotic and macabre and recalls the repetitious and incantatory poetry of Breton, Patchen, and Eluard. Like Barker, Watkins has been criticized for assuming the role of "the priestly bard": Ian Hamilton writes that "Watkins, in particular, is often discovered at the centre of his verse in some quasi-divine posture."[43] But Watkins is in agreement with a "tradition" which "transmits, as surely as Plato or Coleridge or Blake, the doctrine of the 'other' mind of poetic inspiration," Kathleen Raine argues in

"Vernon Watkins. Poet of Tradition." And the "bard is the oracle of that mind, that world. . . ."[44] It is a tradition that not only Hamilton finds objectionable. Noting that Watkins "made a brief sortie into Cambridge as an undergraduate at William Empson's very college, at the time I was myself a student at Griton," Raine remarks on Watkins's "clear-sightedness": "Perhaps he understood even then that tradition has more to give a poet than education has; and perhaps, in the light of that tradition, divined the other great lack in the Cambridge 'scientific' school of literary criticism of Richards, Empson and (already) Leavis, the denial of the living imagination."[45] A point of Raine's essay is that a less anti-imaginative critical perspective would allow a greater valuation of Watkins as a poet. Thomas, whose Neo-Romantic approach to art and experience resembles that of his friend Watkins, once remarked, Raine recounts, that "Watkins was an even better poet than himself, a wonderful poet."[46]

Larkin argues that both the "Apocalyptics" and Watkins were "aiming at ecstasy,"[47] and John Heath-Stubbs argues that "Watkins's vision of life against a background of mythic and archetypal images" is the "only direct relationship between Watkins and the Apocalyptics."[48] More certainly, Watkins, like Read and Jung, senses the apocalyptic significance of war.

In "The Broken Sea," Watkins, like Woodcock in "Waterloo Bridge," begins with a reference to an earlier visionary, Blake, and describes the effects of the War in cataclysmic or apocalyptic imagery borrowed from the Bible or the apocalyptic poetry of nineteenth-century Romantics, such as Blake and Shelley. Telescopic fusions of events seemingly apocalyptic in significance provide a method of enlarging the poem's scope. In particular, Watkins's allusions to the heaven-sent fiery destruction of Sodom and Gomorrah become associated with his allusions to the Holy Spirit in tongues of fire descending on Pentecost and to the fire-bombing Blitz.

Watkins imagery of blood and fire is descended from Joel's vision of wonders in the heavens, such as blood and fire, and similar apocalyptic imagery in St. John's Revelation and Blake's apocalyptic poems, such as *Jerusalem*. Spender's "Epilogue to a Human Drama" (1949) contains similar apocalyptic imagery, as does Hendry's "London Before Invasion."

The doomsday atmosphere of Part V of Eliot's *The Waste Land* probably also influenced Watkins, as well as Thomas, Hendry, and Treece. Thomas's "Author's Prologue" (1952), for example, follows Part V of Eliot's *The Waste Land* in Thomas's images of "towers" (Eliot's "falling towers") like Babel's tower or modern skyscrapers destined for destruction, and conflagration apparently initiated by spontaneous combustion—Eliot's city "burst in the violet air," whereas Thomas describes "cities . . . whose towers will catch/In the religious wind." (The equation fusing Babel's tower and confusion of tongues with modern buildings ignited by the Blitz was contagious: cf. Heath-Stubb's "The False Return" and Bayliss's "Apocalypse and Resurrection.") Eliot's images of "violet air," a variation of the blood-red sky overlaying blue air in previous apocalyptic visions, and question format intended to heighten a sense of impending doom ("What is that sound high in the air" and "What is the city over the mountains/Cracks and reforms and bursts in the violet air/Falling towers. . . ."), may have also proved inspirational to Hendry's "Prelude to a Ballad for Heroes" ("What is that in the bloody as arson sky. . . ."). In any case, such apocalyptic imagery assumes enlarged significance during a world war which seems apocalyptic in scope: the heavens or sky ignited in blood-red fire and smoke becomes, as in Watkins's poem, an expression of a shared vision of London, Dresde, and Berlin ignited in a holocaust by fire-bombing legions of droning aircraft.

"The Broken Sea" also gains its apocalyptic atmosphere through allusions to the first apocalyptic or end-of-the-world catastrophe of the Bible, Noah's deluge.

In "Author's Prologue," Thomas, in a more jocular resurrection of apocalyptic imagery of fire and flood, builds his "bellowing ark / . . . As the flood begins, / Out of the fountainhead / Of fear, rage red, manalive. . . ." Tindall accurately finds Thomas's "fountainhead" as "at once spring and volcano. . . ."[49] But it is also a variation of the Genesis image of the "fountains of the great deep" opening up, although Thomas may have also read Wordsworth's apocalyptic vision in *The Prelude* which presents a vast flash flood as an agent of destruction: Wordsworth describes his Arab seer declaring that it is " 'the waters of the deep / Gathering upon us.' "

Thomas's popular "A Refusal to Mourn the Death, by Fire, of a Child in London" also bears comparison with Watkins's "The Broken

Sea." Thomas begins his poem with a vision of a watery apocalyptic
conclusion to history in which the sea, broken out of its boundaries,
has again been tamed. The poet will not "murder" the "majesty and
burning of the child's death" until creative "darkness / Tells with silence the last light breaking / And the still hour / Is come of the sea
tumbling in harness." But elegiac in spite of himself, Thomas concludes with an ambiguous reference to, among other things, St.
John's apocalyptic vision in Revelation of "no more death." Refusing
to make abstract that which is concrete, to paraphrase Sartre,
Thomas, like Watkins in "The Broken Sea" and Comfort in "Elegy
for a Girl Dead in an Air-Raid," laments the death of a single anon-
ymous child who can represent all the nameless and often innocent
victims of war's slaughter.

Both the poems of Thomas and Watkins echo earlier apocalyptic
visions in which time runs out, is transcended, or shall be no more,
as in St. John's vision in Revelation: Thomas's "still hour." The sense
of time dilating, expanding, or becoming limitless (a temporal equivalent of the sense of vastness, infinity, or limitless space in nineteenth-century apocalyptic poetry) is suggested in Barker's apocalyptic lament, "Elegy No. I." On that "occasion Time / Swells like a
wave at a wall and bursts to eternity." A sense of time collapsing,
diminishing, or dissolving is also part of such visionary poetry and
linked with an existential awareness of death's proximity and the
brevity of human existence (Barker's "time foreshadowing its climax"). In Barker's poem, such an awareness of mortality generates a
seize-the-day attitude, since, in Marvell's language, we sense "Time's
winged chariot hurrying near":

> Lovers on Sunday in the rear seats of cinemas
> Kiss deep and dark, for is it the last kiss?
> Children sailing on swings in municipal parks
> Swing high, swing high into the reach of the sky,
> Leave, leave the sad star that is about to die.
> Laugh, my comedians, who may not laugh again—
>   Soon, soon,
> Soon Jeremiah Job will be walking among men.

Romantic and biblical apocalyptic imagery reappears in the poetry
of the 1930s and the 1940s partly as an anticipation or reflection of

what Breton describes as the unavoidable world catastrophe (*la catastrophe mondiale*). It generally disappears with the end of hostilities which also conclude the prophetic function of the poet whose prophecies have largely become realized. Tom Scott, associated with the New Apocalypse, expressed the seemingly unavoidable writer's block for the visionary poet: ". . . the real apocalypse which broke on us in the actual war was so colossal as to completely swamp our warnings in verse. That led to my drying up pending getting a new direction. But the apocalypse really happened as all history knows."[50] Gascoyne's view is similar: "Well, I anticipated the war which actually happened. But then after the war was over, there was nothing better. And then there was an awful sort of let down after that. And then I became silent for many years. And now there's a great deal of apprehension again. I mean, who could avoid it?"[51]

Indeed. Who could avoid it? And herein may lie part of the relevancy of apocalyptic poetry beyond the context of the impending and actual catastrophe which generated such poetry. It is partly of interest because we have incorporated into our thinking the seemingly inescapable and unending possibility of an apocalyptic conclusion to world history. Whereas the 1930s constitute "a low dishonest decade," the 1940s, as the art of Read and the Neo-Romantics reminds us, constitute a decade still lower and in many ways more dishonest. It is the most violent, destructive decade of human history. The "holocaust" in which millions of innocent persons were exterminated, the development of the concept of total war applied to the fire-bombing of London and Dresden, the explosion of the first atomic bombs and subsequent development of nuclear arsenals and a balance-of-terror military philosophy, have all become part of the popular imagination.

Chapter Seven
Conclusion
After Neo-Romanticism

In *A New Romantic Anthology,* the last Neo-Romantic collection of writings, Read writes of the " 'rehabilitation of romanticism' as an adequate description" of his "aim."[1] His ideas on art, politics, and education, and his literary criticism (Wordsworth, for example—"no one had ever written so revealingly of Wordsworth," Graham Greene believed),[2] contributed to such an objective. But Read's ideas about the principles of art and poetry provided less support for what Charles Tomlinson describes as the "impulsive," "unchecked" rhetoric of "Neo-Romanticism in general and of the New Apocalyptics in particular."[3] The fire-watch was over and Cassandra's shrill voice was silenced. A concerted reaction against Apocalypticism and Neo-Romanticism was about to begin.

New Lines. Some cynicism about Neo-Romantic flights of the imagination may be at work at the conclusion of the last Apocalyptic anthology, *The Crown and the Sickle* (1944), in Terence White's "Some Proverbs for the Age": "He who flies highest may not have the best parachute."[4] But it was the poets of the so-called Movement of the 1950s who most decisively reacted against Apocalypticism and the larger Neo-Romanticism.

Robert Conquest in his "introduction" to *New Lines: An Anthology* (1956), which he edited, provides a rationale for the Movement. "In the 1940s," Conquest writes, "the mistake was made of giving the Id, a sound player on the percussion side under a strict conductor, too much of a say in the doings of the orchestra as a whole." Ironically, Conquest's argument for the anti-Romantic Movement is basically the same as Hendry's argument in the first two paragraphs of his Introduction to *The New Apocalypse.* Apocalyptic poetry is intended for the "whole personality," Hendry argues, and Apocalyptic writing transcends modern "pathological" systems to provide a "cure." Arguing for a "healthy" viewpoint, Conquest writes of the "restoration" of "the principle that poetry is written by and for the whole man, intellect, emotions, sense and all."[5]

Kingsley Amis in "Against Romanticism" in Conquest's anthology analyzes the problems of the Apocalyptic and Neo-Romantic writers and presents a solution: "To please an ingrown taste for anarchy / Torrid images circle in the wood," while "Over all, a grand meaning fills the scene, / And sets the brain raging with prophecy. . . . Better, of course if images were plain. . . ." Read would not have totally disagreed with Amis. The qualities of discipline, precision, and concision—usually apparent in his own Imagist poetry—are often absent from Apocalyptic and Neo-Romantic art.

Moreover, the sort of prophetic, exhortatory style and tone of the Apocalyptic anthologies in particular were not well suited to the postwar world (it would have been like having Blake or Carlyle transported into the 1950s) and its generally less radical poets.

Amis in "Against Romanticism" defends in effect the Classical ideals of urban moderation and democracy from Neo-Romantic excess, anarchism, fascination with Nature, and Surrealistic images:

> A traveller who walks a temperate zone
> —Wood devoid of beasts, roads that please the foot—
> Finds that its decent surface grows too thin:
> Something unperceived fumbles at his nerves.
> To please an ingrown taste for anarchy
> Torrid images circle in the wood. . . .

In place of Neo-Romantic obscurity, symbolic indefiniteness and complexity, and utopian visionariness, Amis argues for Classical lucidity, plainness, and practicality:

> Better, of course, if images were plain,
> Warnings clearly said, . . .
> But complexities crowd the simplest thing,
> And flaw the surface that they cannot break.

The Second World War seemed argument enough that more emphasis should be placed on comprehensibility and communication, and an emphasis on semantics, replacing the older interest in a common language system, Esperanto, emerged in the 1950s. The *New Lines* reaction to Neo-Romanticism implied also a preference for reason over imagination. It is not that Movement poets recapture the relatively naive faith of Neo-Classical poets in human rationality. Like the Neo-Romantics, they are under the influence of Freud, but Freud the rationalist—a fact some Neo-Romantics and Surrealists tend to ignore—who aimed at subduing irrationality and demonstrated its dangerous extent in human affairs.

Like Neo-Classical Poetry, the poetry of the Movement, whether intentionally or not, expresses symbolically its preference for common sense and rationality. Neo-Romantic literature is permeated by darkness and underground imagery, symbolic of the unconscious—as in Lawrence's "Bavarian Gentians" or Read's Part Three of *The Green Child*. In contrast, *New Lines* poetry contains images of light and air or sky, which express, among other things, fascination with clarity, rationality, and lucidity.

Clearing the air for more rational, less politically leftist, communication, Amis declares in "Against Romanticism," "Let the sky be clean of officious birds / Punctiliously flying on the left. . . ." Amis's pronouncements recall those of Jehovah creating, out of a murky, amorphous world, "without form and void," an ordered, illuminated environment: "Let there be light. . . ." But awesome pronouncement or rational argument against Apocalypticism and Neo-Romanticism were not actually necessary. In MacCaig's language in "Birds All Singing," "Time topples bird and man out of their myth."

Romantic anarchists like Shelley, Read, Gardiner, and Treece are open to the charge by liberals and conservatives of having no institutional programs to effect social change. Amis argues that Romantics—preoccupied with a "grand meaning" rather than with mundane details, a political base for corporate action, or realizable goals—rage

> to build a better time and place
> Than the ones which give prophecy its field
> To work, the calm material for its rage,
> And the context which makes it prophecy.
>
> Let us make at least visions that we need. . . .

Movement poets, like Neo-Classicists, also objected to the Romantic and Neo-Romantic expressions of powerful feelings or strong emotion in verse. The expression of such emotions does not characterize Neo-Classical and Movement poetry partly because the expression of strong personal emotions allows vulnerability, whereas escape from personality and revelation of private feelings, through ironic detachment, functions to protect the hidden self by removing it from ridicule or analysis. In addition, Movement poets, partly reacting against what they perceived to be the political naiveté and personal irrationality of Romantics and Neo-Romantics, placed a relatively greater value on reason rather than emotion or intuition in the decision-making process. Both anarchism and nineteenth- and twentieth-century Romanticism contain strong biases toward rationalism and, in anarchism, especially, the scientific method; like Luther's inner light, individual reason, in Godwin and Read, takes the place of external authority, and the scientific method, the place of traditional dogma.

But in general, Romanticism and anarchism—which coalesce in Shelley, the major Apocalyptics, and the Neo-Romantics—imply, in the language of Wrey Gardiner's "Poem for the Sane," that "We are unwise to decry the wisdom of the heart. . . ." Both strong emotionality and fascination with irrational modes of perception sometimes contribute to the self-destructive tendencies of nineteenth- and twentieth-century Romantics, leading to partial disillusionment: "I have been told to reason by the heart,/But heart, like head, leads helplessly," writes Thomas, probably paraphrasing Pascal, in "Should Lanterns Shine."

Moreover, Classical and Neo-Classical writers are generally more preoccupied with social roles than are Romantic and Neo-Romantic writers, and such a preoccupation contributes to sexual polarization and male domination. Lacking the androgyny awareness of Romantics such as Shelley and Read, such writers are likely to conclude that only a woman would be foolish enough to risk exposure by expressing strong personal feelings in art. In Kingsley Amis's "A Bookshop Idyll," Amis finds that poems

> . . . divide by sex:
> *Landscape near Parma*
> Interest a man, so does *The Double Vortex,*
> So does *Rilke and Buddha.*

The ladies' choice, discountenance my patter . . .

Should poets bicycle-pump the human heart
  Or squash it flat?
Man's love is of man's life a thing apart;
  Girls aren't like that.

What is divided by sex, no man should put together, and the choice
of terms—"patter," "Man's" versus "Girls"—announces the direction
of sexual bias. But the primary point here is that Amis, after noting
that women are inclined to "write about it" [love], adds,

And the awful way their poems lay them open
  Just doesn't strike them.
Women are really much nicer than men:
  No wonder we like them.

Such patronizing irony and wit are linked with the disturbing truth
that male poets, inhibited by a society which thinks the direct
expression of emotion feminine (and therefore weak, silly, and em-
barrassing), run against writer's block: "Deciding this, we can forget
those times / We sat up half the night / Chock-full of love, crammed
with bright thoughts, names, rhymes, / And couldn't write."

Like public revelation of strong personal emotions, forthright commitment to socially unacceptable causes is generally absent from
Movement poetry. But cold-war politics, damning Neo-Romantic anarchism through McCarthyian guilt by association, also made commitment by intellectuals to radical politics dangerous and detachment
a survival mechanism among poets too sensitive or sensible simply to
be propagandists for establishment attitudes. Aloofness, the antithesis
of Neo-Romantic rebellion against authority and Existentialistic en-
gagement, manifested itself in a detached presentation of verbal complexity, wit, irony, and awareness of multiple points of view which,
among other things, rationalizes for the self and others noncommit-
ment and defends the poet and poetry against attack. Attracted to
their opposites, committed Christians and alienated Beatniks, the
armchair cyclists of the 1950s could discover themselves standing am-
bivalently before tradition, "Hatless," taking off "cycle-clips in awk-
ward reverence" (in Larkin's popular "Church Going").

In place of Neo-Romantic introspection and impressionistic responses to Nature, Movement poets valued extrospection and essentially realistic reflections of the urban environment. The "inward gaze" or "inward eye" is replaced by a new respect for the camera's eye, recalling Neo-Classicism's respect for the telescope and astronomy. Treece in "To the Edge and Back" had been informed in a vision that the "eyes" of the "Bard" are "not the reasonable cameras of ordinary men. . . ." Larkin, on the other hand, acknowledges in "Lines on a Young Lady's Photograph Album" the supremacy in one respect, at least, of photography over art:

> O, photography! as no art is,
> Faithful and disappointing! that records
> Dull days as dull, and hold-it smiles as frauds,
> And will not censor blemishes. . . .
> . . . what grace
> Your candour thus confers. . . .
> How overwhelmingly persuades
> That this is a real girl in a real place.

In "Against Romanticism" Amis, from a similar perspective, castigates Romanticism for "Raging to discard real time and place. . . ."

"But dreams know no time nor fixed degree of space," in the language of Wrey Gardiner's "The Gates of Silence." From the Romanticist's perspective, "dream time," encompassing timeless archetypes and acknowledging the relativity of time as subjectively experienced, is also real, and the terrains of Gardiner's "Landscape of the Mind," Treece's "land no eye has seen," and Hendry's "shores no eye may see," also have reality.

While emphasizing the external environment, Movement poets also emphasized the here and now. Both in a physical and chronological sense, the immediate environment is the subject of Larkin's "Here." His "Triple Time" gives priority to the present—"This empty street, this sky to blandness scoured, / This air"—which, unlike past or future psychological orientations, includes the two other dimensions of time, "the future furthest childhood saw," and the "past" ("And on another day will be the past . . ."). Conscious receptivity to the environment, in contrast to the emphasis of some Neo-Romantics on "dream time," allows our perception of present, past, and future to be integrated meaningfully; in the language of the poem, by attending to the present, we become possessors of "triple time," certainly a psychological coup or three-base hit.

Preoccupation with the future, like Neo-Romantic visionary utopianism or sense of impending doom, may be debilitating, Larkin's poetry suggests, or may leave the poet or his reader feeling empty, for the resources of the present environment are sidestepped as fretting about the future becomes obsessive. Larkin in "Next, Please" dissects such a disease of the imagination, finding that it wastes life and time before death, the only human expectancy that matters. In contrast, Gardiner in *The Once Loved God* writes pejoratively of "this worn door-step we call here and now."[6]

But preoccupation with vicarious rather than real experience, as in Romantic medievalism, and obsession with catharsis, or Freudian regurgitation of childhood, produce through the deprivations and pain involved their own kind of backlash, evident in Barker's ambivalence toward obsessive introspection and preoccupation with the past in his "The True Confessions of George Barker": "For God's sake, Barker. This is enough / Regurgitated obscenities, Whimsicalities and such stuff." The historical oscillations between Classicism and Romanticism, including that between Neo-Romanticism and Movement poetry, are partly the product of the mind's own self-limiting tendency. Satiated with introspection, the Neo-Romantics generally move on their own, without *New Lines* direction, away from subjectivity toward objectivity and the immediate environment.

But it is also a matter of relative emphasis. For Read, wholeness involves immediacy of experience, a sense of the here and now, which conceptual thought tends to block. Libertarian writers, such as Woodcock, Comfort, and Patchen, are from the outset responsive in their poetry to the present environment. Woodcock's "Now (for Elizabeth)" anticipates Larkin's "Here" and Amis's "Against Romanticism" in reacting against debilitating preoccupation with the past or future. The present, although precarious, is the environment that matters most, and dialogue, as an aspect of the fusional quality of romantic love, is a means of alleviating anxiety about the fulfillment of apocalyptic prophecies of universal disaster:

> Now I compare the forecasts with events,
> Noting the lucky prophesy of each seer,

It is no calm of courage in the spring
That has outdriven my autumn fear.

It is no certainty of hiding safe
From steel or the conscripting hand of death
Swells my serenity like a tube of peace
Lipped to the wet staunchness of the earth.

Only the pattern of your wishing parts
me so from fate. . . .

You are invisible friendship in this forest,
Warning the shadows and the bladder ogres. . . .

You, speaking and silent with me, and loved
Here and away, make Now a lucky land. . . .

But Now, authentic Phoenix, dies as lives.
Now lasts only an instant. Now is land
Where the events are, Now is not event.
And when the events attack, what walls shall stand?

Developments in psychology during and after the war help to
account for a decreasing interest in the sort of preoccupation with introspection which characterizes Apocalypticism. Psychoanalysis was
becoming more ego, rather than id, oriented, and Fromm's Neo-
Freudianism emphasized sociological and political, rather than childhood, determinants of neurosis. Skinner's *Walden Two* (1948) popularized a new form of Behaviorism, operant conditioning, which
stressed action in, or operation upon, the environment, rather than
conditioning, after Pavlov and Watson, through the autonomic nervous system. Fritz Perls's Gestaltism emphasized the present, the
"now," as did Ellis's Rational-Emotive Therapy. Existentialism, in-
fluencing Rollo May, Abraham Maslow, and Carl Rogers, also directed the focus of concern to the individual's present experience of
"being-in-the-world," rather than on the past. It is the phenomenological basis of Existentialism which partly accounts for its less past-
obsessed vision. But religious or Freudian and Jungian wallowing in
the past, individual or societal, is escapist and irresponsible for Ca-

mus and Sartre. Eysenck in the 1950s exploded a bombshell by providing statistical evidence that psychoanalysis produced no significant improvements over those gained without any psychotherapy through spontaneous remissions, thereby casting in doubt the therapeutic benefits to be gained through art which exposes the unconscious origins of neurosis.

The environment had also changed. With postwar prosperity and the absence of world war, poets were less motivated to escape from the present into a personal or historical past, as in Treece's medievalism. Boredom, rather than terror, emerges as a theme in Movement poetry. Fantasies of escaping, with Gauguin aplomb, into an idealized external environment and subculture life-style—rather than into the recesses of the psyche or the past or future—become the price-tag for seemingly adult acceptance of the here and now, common sense, and common morality. In "Toads" Larkin finds everyday, meaningless work oppressive: "Why should I let the toad *work* / Squat on my life?" But he answers himself, "Ah, were I courageous enough / To shout *Stuff your pension!* / But I know, all too well, that's the stuff / That dreams are made on. . . ." The reference seems to be not to Shakespeare, but to Humphrey Bogart's paraphrase of Shakespeare at the conclusion of *The Maltese Falcon* (1941), which, in its depiction of a cynical urban "hero," provides 1950s poets a model for identification in escapist fantasies.

Similarly, in "Poetry of Departures," Larkin, still meditating on the possibility of escape, finds the notion of escape from an artificial, object-oriented, stultifying, and impersonal society to be itself "artificial, / Such a deliberate step backwards / To create an object: / Books; china, a life / Reprehensibly perfect." What he describes, however, is the escape artist's perfection of the *role,* rather than the possibility of moving into a less inhibited, more spontaneous, essentially roleless mode of existence. The ideal mode of "Triple Time," life lived fully engaged in the present, redeeming past and future, is the sort of perfection longed for but difficult to achieve in the social role-playing decade of The-Man-in-the-Gray-Flannel-Suit.

In "Toads Revisited," Larkin revisits the middle-class burden of repressive labor, finding the life-style of those in an urban park who dodge such work representative of escape from one intolerable environment into another. Such unemployed characters,

> All dodging the toad work
> By being stupid or weak.
> Think of being them!
> Hearing the hours chime
> Watching the bread delivered,
> The sun by clouds covered,
> The children going home;
> Think of being them. . . .

Despite the limitations of his imagination, Larkin's poetry is refreshingly honest, and its honesty and relevancy to everyday existence are a source of its appeal in the 1950s. Most readers, including highly literate and sophisticated readers, do not see visions, or find credible those who do, or dream fantastic Jungian or Freudian dreams; most do work daily and can identify with a poet who writes about work, as Larkin does. It is an imaginative deficiency of the Apocalyptics, especially, to fail to redeem the city by treating realistic, practical alternatives to urban ennui and occupational boredom.

But *New Lines* poets are not consciously or unconsciously following the same literary models. Apocalyptic mentality, whether first-, nineteenth-, or twentieth-century, inhibits interest in ordinary activities, such as ordinary work and domesticity. In addition, we should not forget, in Hendry's language, "the bomb and the terror." In the 1940s the urban environments the Neo-Romantics knew were being threatened, partly evacuated, and later partly destroyed by the Blitz.

Some of the poets of the 1940s felt alienated from British society, as well as threatened by it: on 12 December 1945, the government raided the Freedom Press, and shortly thereafter arrested for sedition three anarchists connected with it. (A protest was signed by T. S. Eliot, E. M. Forster, the anarchist Ethel Mannin, John Middleton Murry, Herbert Read, and others and printed in the *New Statesman and Nation* on 3 March 1945.) Understandably, some anarchists and sympathizing libertarian pacifists, such as Patchen, felt they had much in common with persecuted European writers, such as Paul Éluard and Jean Giono. The rhetoric of Patchen's "I DON'T WANT TO STARTLE YOU but they are going to kill most of us" and angry litanies of Patchen's *Journal of Albion Moonlight* (part of which is anthologized in *New Road*) and Comfort's "None But My Foe to Be My

Guide" find their analogues in Éluard's *Poésie et Vérité* [Poetry and Truth, 1942] and Giono's *Refusal to Obey*:

> There is only one single remedy: our strength. There is only
>   one single way of using it: revolt.
> Since our voices have not been heard.
> Since our moans have not been heeded.
> Since they have turned away when we have shown the wounds
>   of our hands, our feet, our foreheads.
> Since, without pity, they bring again the crown of thorns,
>   and already see there prepared the nails and the hammer.

Refusal to Obey was anthologized in *New Road*, as well as, earlier, in Savage's *Phoenix*.

Post–Neo-Romantic Continuations.   In the year that Read was knighted and appointed Charles Eliot Norton Professor of Poetry at Harvard, 1953, he was discontent. Spender recalls a luncheon with Read at The Saville on 30 January 1953: "He is depressed by an overwhelming sense of decay, and by loss of faith in the social ideas—and perhaps the aesthetic theories—which have kept him going all his life." Read mentioned the families in Yorkshire "crippled by having to pay death duties." Spender said, ". . . I thought income tax was really better and that we were living through a transition time in which we combined the evils of capitalism with those of collectivist bureaucracy." Read was subsequently "cheered up a bit," but not for long: " 'Everything is dead,' he said at some point in the conversation, and I think really this is what he thinks now."[7]

The 1950s made other antiestablishment writers look back in anger born of the same frustration or howl against depersonalization by conformist society. But the matter does not stop there. In Read's language, everything was not dead. Some trends were hibernating. They extend into the 1960s and 1970s the preoccupations of radicals and liberals in the 1940s. Comfort's *Barbarism and Sexual Freedom* (1943) and *Sex in Society* (1950) foreshadow his libertarian *The Joy of Sex* (1972). They foreshadowed also the sexual revolution of Marxist Herbert Marcuse, Wilhelm Reich, and Albert Ellis. Such a preoccupation with the establishment of rational attitudes toward sexual behavior and with the emancipation of women, as in the works of Emma

Goldman and Mary Wollstonecraft Godwin, is fundamental to anarchist and libertarian thought.

Existentialism also helped in reviving Neo-Romantic concerns. Camus's *The Rebel* was translated into English with a "Foreword" by Herbert Read (1956), who accurately notes that "Camus's ideas come close to anarchism. . . ."[8] Both Existentialism and Neo-Romanticism focus on subjectivity; purposelessness or the anomic disintegration of absolute values; depersonalization and the dehumanizing effects of external control; and Promethean, individual, rather than essentially collective, modes of rebellion and social change. Both share an antipathy toward abstractions; in Neo-Romanticism it is partly the product of the influence of earlier anarchists, such as Kropotkin, and the anticonceptual bias of Surrealism. Like Neo-Romanticism, French Existentialism in particular is in a sense also a revelation of last things, death and destruction, and an analogous philosophy of individuality, crisis, and anxiety and terror. It shares with Neo-Romanticism an antipathy toward mass behavior, to "the roaring masses who belch their way towards . . . oblivion," in the angry language of Gardiner in *The Flowering Moment*.[9]

Also revived after the war is the sort of concern for the development of a "Social Pathology," as Hendry calls it in a letter of 24 August 1940 to Treece, that Hendry, Comfort, and Read wanted to bring about. The sense that coercive society is psychopathological is pervasive in anarchist thought and reflected in the anarchist writings of Hendry, Rexroth, Goodman, Woodcock, and Read. On the other hand, the popular image of the anarchist, as in Conrad's *The Secret Agent,* Chesterton's *The Man Who Was Thursday,* and James's *The Princess Casamassima,* is that of the anarchist as madman or as mentally disturbed because suffering from feelings of inferiority.

The development of a social psychopathology of necessity involves the clarification and repudiation of the normative assumptions of adjustment psychology. If "society [rather than the maladjusted individual] is neurotic," Hendry argues, then ". . . it would be a pity, if not a calamity, were the individual to adapt himself to it."[10] More recently, R. D. Laing in his psychiatric *The Politics of Experience* (1967) asks, "Adaptation to what? To Society? To a world gone mad?"[11] Adjustment psychology is also the target of Huxley's *Brave*

New World (1932), Kesey's *One Flew Over the Cuckoo's Nest* (1962), and Burgess's *A Clockwork Orange* (1962), all of which also focus on another central anarchist and Neo-Romantic concern, the mechanization of human existence.

Other Neo-Romantic concerns reappear in the counter-culture ideologies and psychological therapies (of Fritz Perls, Paul Goodman, Rogers, etc.) of the 1960s and 1970s. The androgyny interests of Shelley and Read (psychological wholeness involves the fusion of male and female—the Green Child—principles) anticipate those of the anarchic New Left of the 1960s. Preoccupation with the dangers of technology, depersonalization by the machinery of institutions, and decentralization characterizes also New-Left thinking, which, like British anarchism and Neo-Romanticism in the 1940s, is partly born out of cynicism about political leaders and war and is diminished by the end of a war provided a rallying point, as well as by the cooptation of counterculture norms by the dominant society.

Notes and References

Chapter One

1. Letter from Nicholas Moore, 19 August 1980.
2. Letter from Moore, 9 September 1980.
3. Ibid.
4. Ibid.
5. Letter from Moore, 19 August 1980.
6. Letter from Moore, 9 September 1980.
7. Note from James F. Hendry, 6 October 1980.
8. Conversation with Hendry, 3 October 1980.
9. Ibid.
10. Ibid.
11. Letter from Moore, 9 September 1980.
12. Hendry's 5 January 1939 letter to Treece.
13. Note from Hendry, 6 October 1980.
14. Letter from Comfort, 28 August 1980.
15. Ibid.
16. Letter from Hendry, 14 November 1980.
17. This and all the subsequent letters to Comfort have been graciously provided by Joseph W. Scott, Librarian, from the Comfort collection of correspondence and publications of the University College, University of London.
18. Discussion with Hendry, 3 October 1980.
19. Wrey Gardiner letter received 14 October 1980.
20. See *Poetry* 69, no. 6 (March 1947):299–349.
21. Gardiner's 14 October 1980 letter.
22. Ibid.
23. Conversation with Roland Gant, January 1982. Baker, as Gant notes, "took to drink" in the early 1950s and was sent to prison for seven years for embezzling 750,000 pounds.
24. Ibid.
25. Moore's 6 November 1980 letter. Seeing narrow exclusiveness in Geoffrey Grigson's *New Verse* and Julian Symons's *Twentieth Century Verse,* Tambi attempted to "break their monopoly," in his words (January 1982, conversation with Tambi). As Derek Stanford notes in *Inside the Forties: Literary Memoirs 1937–1957* (London: Sidgwick & Jackson, 1977), Moore was

"ensconced as Tambimuttu's number one in *Poetry* London's Manchester Square Sanctum" (p. 87).

26. Letter from George Woodcock, 17 September 1980.

27. Comfort's 28 August 1980 letter.

28. Ibid.

29. Woodcock's 17 September 1980 letter.

30. Moore's 9 September 1980 letter.

31. Hendry's 6 October 1980 note.

32. Comfort's 28 August 1980 letter.

33. Letter from Gardiner, 22 November 1980.

34. Stephen Spender, *The Thirties and After: Poetry, Politics, People, 1933–1970* (New York: Random House, 1978), p. 7.

35. Conversation with Comfort, 7 August 1974.

36. Comfort's 28 August 1980 letter.

37. Moore's 19 August 1980 letter.

38. Gardiner's 14 October 1980 letter.

39. Charles Mortiz, ed., *Current Biography Yearbook* (New York: H. W. Wilson, 1962), p. 347.

40. George Woodcock, *Herbert Read: The Stream and the Source* (London: Faber, 1972), p. 28.

41. G. S. Fraser, "Apocalypse in Poetry," in *The White Horseman,* ed. J. F. Hendry and Henry Treece (London, 1941), p. 29.

42. Herbert Read, *The Cult of Sincerity* (New York: Horizon Press, 1969), p. 103.

43. Ibid., pp. 105, 101.

44. Ibid., p. 104.

45. Herbert Read, *The Contrary Experience* (New York: Faber and Faber, 1963), p. 71.

46. Ibid., p. 75.

47. Ibid., p. 87.

48. Read, *Cult of Sincerity,* p. 107.

49. Ibid., p. 108.

50. Ibid., p. 112.

51. William York Tindall, *Forces in Modern British Literature: 1885–1956* (New York: Vintage Books, 1947), p. 90.

52. Woodcock, *Herbert Read,* p. 23.

53. Stephen Spender, *World Within World: The Autobiography of Stephen Spender* (Berkeley: University of California Press, 1966), p. 95.

54. Woodcock, *Herbert Read,* p. 86.

55. Read, *Cult of Sincerity,* pp. 152–53.

56. Ibid., p. 174.

57. Henry Treece, ed., *Herbert Read: An Introduction to His Work by Various Hands* (London: Faber and Faber, 1944), p. 15.

58. T. E. Hulme, "Romanticism and Classicism," in *Critiques and Essays in Criticism,* ed. Robert Stallman (New York: Ronald Press Co., 1949), p. 6.

59. Treece, ed., *Herbert Read,* p. 15.

60. Fraser, "Apocalypse in Poetry," p. 17.

61. Spender, *World Within World,* p. 95.

62. Amitava Banerjee, *Spirit Above Wars: A Study of the English Poetry of the Two World Wars* (Delhi: MacMillan Co. of India, 1975), pp. 98–99.

63. Graham Greene, "A Personal Foreword" to Read's *The Contrary Experience,* p. 7.

64. C. G. Jung, *Memories, Dreams, Reflections,* ed. Aniela Jaffe (New York: Vintage Books, 1961), pp. 181–82.

65. Ibid., pp. 159–60.

66. Wrey Gardiner, *The Once Loved God: A Landscape of the Mind* (London, 1943), p. 3.

67. Fraser, "Apocalypse in Poetry," p. 29.

68. Norman MacCaig, *Far Cry* (London: Routledge, 1943), p. 7.

69. Hulme, "Romanticism and Classicism," p. 4.

70. Fraser, "Apocalypse in Poetry," p. 52.

71. Note from Hendry, 6 October 1980.

72. Woodcock, *Herbert Read,* p. 26.

73. Tindall, *Forces in Modern British Literature,* p. 236.

74. Tindall, *A Reader's Guide to Dylan Thomas* (New York: Farrar, Straus and Cudahy, 1962), p. 10.

75. Tindall, *Forces in Modern British Literature,* p. 237.

76. Walford Morgan, *A New Romantic Anthology* (London: Grey Walls Press, 1949), pp. 54–55.

77. See Treece's *How I See Apocalypse* (London: L. Drummond, 1946), p. 175, and Fraser's "Apocalypse in Poetry," p. 3.

78. George Orwell, "The Dark Horse of the Apocalypse," *Life and Letters To-Day* 25 (June 1940):315.

79. Fraser, "Apocalypse in Poetry," pp. 4–5.

80. Conversation with David Gascoyne, 27 March 1981.

81. Conversation with John Bayliss, January 1982.

82. Carl Sagan, *The Dragons of Eden: Speculations on the Evolution of Human Intelligence* (New York: Ballantine Books, 1977), pp. 98, 99, 146.

83. Ibid., p. 150.

84. Revelation 12:3.

85. Revelation 13:1.

86. Revelation 15:2.
87. Jung, *Memories,* pp. 181, 182.
88. Revelation 5:1.
89. Revelation 20:1–2.

Chapter Two

1. The 22 December 1938 letter from Thomas to Goodland.
2. Letter from Moore, 9 October 1980.
3. Frederick J. Hoffman, "From Surrealism to 'The Apocalypse': A Development in Twentieth Century Irrationalism," *Journal of English Library History* 15 (1948):148.
4. Jo Ann Baggerly, "Henry Treece and the New Apocalypse: A Study of English Neo-Romanticism," Ph.D. diss., Texas Technological University, 1973, p. 3.
5. Note from Hendry, 6 October 1980.
6. D. H. Lawrence, *Apocalypse* (New York: Viking Press, 1931), p. 51.
7. Spender, *The Thirties and After,* p. 11.
8. André Breton, *Manifestes Du Surréalisme* (Paris: Gallimard, n.d.), p. 67.
9. William Wordsworth, *The Prelude,* book V, ll. 78–79.
10. "An Interview with George Barker," conducted by Cyrena Pondrom on 9 September 1970, in *Contemporary Literature,* Autumn 1971, p. 382.
11. Ibid., pp. 382–83.
12. Letter from Moore, 9 September 1980.
13. Recorded conversation with Hendry, 3 October 1980.
14. Friedrich Nietzsche, *The Joyful Wisdom,* tr. T. Common, from *The Complete Works of Friedrich Nietzsche,* ed. O. Levy (London: T. N. Foulis, 1910), section 125.
15. Recorded conversation, 3 October 1980.
16. Ibid.
17. Letter from Hendry, 14 November 1980.
18. Hendry's 6 October 1980 note.
19. Hendry, *The White Horseman,* p. 225.
20. Recorded conversation, 3 October 1980.
21. Ibid.
22. Page numbers are not included since quotations appearing here are from Hendry's handwritten "Journal," which he graciously allowed me to use.
23. Ibid.
24. Ibid.
25. Ibid.

26. Ibid.

27. Ibid.

28. Ibid.

29. The letter was graciously provided by Mr. Hendry.

30. Letter from Hendry, 14 November 1980.

31. Ibid.

32. T. H. Helmstadter, "The Apocalyptic Movement in British Poetry," Ph.D. diss., University of Pennsylvania, 1963, p. 69.

33. J. F. Hendry, *The Orchestral Mountain: A Symphonic Elegy* (London, 1943), pp. 26–27.

34. Helmstadter, "Apocalyptic Movement," p. 69.

35. Luke 19:37–40.

36. John Bunyan, *The Pilgrim's Progress* (New York: Washington Square Press, 1957), p. 9.

37. Ibid., p. 153.

38. Revelation 14:1–8.

39. Hendry, *Orchestral Mountain,* p. 17.

40. Helmstadter, "Apocalyptic Movement," p. 71.

41. Leviticus 25:2.

42. Revelation 21:1–5.

43. Luke 18:24–25.

44. J. F. Hendry, *The Bombed Happiness* (London, 1942), pp. 15–16. Most of the poems discussed are included in this volume.

45. J. F. Hendry and Henry Treece, eds., *The Crown and the Sickle* (London, 1944), p. 54.

46. Matthew 13:57.

47. Lawrence, *Apocalypse,* pp. 127–28.

48. Ibid., pp. 130, 129.

49. Ibid., p. 129.

Chapter Three

1. Treece, *How I See Apocalypse,* p. 1.

2. Treece's letter to Comfort is from the Comfort collection of the University College, London (see above).

3. Letter from Moore, 9 September 1980.

4. J. C. Chevalier, "Denton Welch—Henry Treece: Une Correspondence," *Etudes Anglaises* 27 (1974):285.

5. Henry Treece, *Dylan Thomas: "Dog Among the Fairies"* (London: Ernest Benn, 1949), pp. 120–21.

6. William York Tindall, *A Reader's Guide to Dylan Thomas* (New York: Farrar, Straus and Cudahy, 1962), p. 54.

7. Herbert Read, *Anarchy and Order: Essays in Politics* (Boston: Beacon Press, 1954), pp. 142–43.

8. Treece, *How I See Apocalypse,* p. 10.

9. Wordsworth, *Prelude,* book V, ll. 143, 145.

10. Elder Olson, *The Poetry of Dylan Thomas* (Chicago: University of Chicago Press, 1954), p. 60.

11. Ibid., pp. 17–18, 21, 23.

12. Ibid., p. 42.

13. Wordsworth, *Prelude,* book V, l. 138.

14. "Notes on Contemporary Tendencies," in *A New Romantic Anthology,* p. 55.

15. Derek Stanford, review of *The Black Seasons, Poetry Quarterly* 7 (Spring 1945):29–30.

16. Alex Comfort, review of *The White Horseman, Poetry Quarterly* 3 (Autumn 1941):81–82.

17. Hendry, *White Horseman,* p. 39.

18. Henry Treece, *The Black Seasons* (London, 1945), p. 40; see pp. 40–44.

19. Helmstadter, "Apocalyptic Movement," p. 136.

20. Graciously provided by Hendry from his personal files.

21. Baggerly, "Henry Treece," p. 95.

22. Helmstadter, "Apocalyptic Movement," pp. 136–37.

23. Treece, *How I See Apocalypse,* p. 19.

24. Cf. Baggerly, "Henry Treece," p. 116.

25. Treece, *New Romantic Anthology,* p. 18.

26. Treece, *New Apocalypse,* p. 49.

27. Ibid., p. 55.

Chapter Four

1. J. F. Hendry, "The Apocalyptic Element in Modern Poetry," *Poetry Scotland,* Second Collection (1945), p. 64.

2. Treece, *How I See Apocalypse,* p. 175.

3. Francis Scarfe, *Auden and After: The Liberation of Poetry, 1930–1941* (London: Routledge, 1942), p. 159.

4. Norman MacCaig, *Far Cry,* (London: Routledge, 1943), p. 18.

5. Ibid., pp. 5, 7, 9.

6. Ibid., p. 6.

7. Ibid., pp. 9–10.

8. Ibid., pp. 5, 13.

9. Ibid., p. 24.

10. Ibid., p. 7.

11. Ibid., p. 13.

12. Ibid., p. 14.

13. Charles Tomlinson, in *The Modern Age,* vol. 7 of the *Pelican Guide to English Literature,* ed. Boris Ford (Baltimore: Penguin, 1963), p. 472.

14. Helmstadter, "Apocalyptic Movement," p. 248.

15. Letter from MacCaig, 15 April 1981.

16. Norman MacCaig, *Riding Lights* (London: Hogarth Press, 1955), p. 29.

17. Ibid., pp. 48–49.

18. Letters from MacCaig, 15 April and 23 February 1981.

19. Scarfe, *Auden and After,* p. 155.

20. Letter from Hendry, 3 November 1980.

21. Letter from Paddy Fraser, 28 July 1980.

22. Letter from Moore, 8 August 1980.

23. Part of the Today and Tomorrow Series (Tokyo: Eibunsha, n.d.), p. iv.

24. Ibid., p. 26.

25. Ibid., pp. 3–4.

26. T. S. Eliot, "Tradition and the Individual Talent," in *Critiques and Essays in Criticism,* pp. 383, 381.

27. G. S. Fraser, *Three Philosophical Essays* (Tokyo, n.d.), p. 2.

28. Ibid., pp. 4–5.

29. Ibid., p. 7.

30. Ibid., p. 43.

31. Ibid., pp. 43–44.

32. Ibid., pp. 4, 45–46.

33. H. M. Abrams, *The Mirror and the Lamp* (New York: W. W. Norton & Co., 1953), p. 59.

34. Ibid., pp. 58–59.

35. Fraser, *Three Philosophical Essays,* p. 45.

36. Ibid., pp. 50–51.

37. G. S. Fraser, *Leaves Without a Tree* (Tokyo, 1953), p. 71.

38. Ibid., p. 69.

39. Ibid., p. 66.

40. Ibid., p. vi.

41. Ibid., p. 24.

42. Ibid.

43. Ibid., p. 11.

44. Letter from Gardiner, 22 November 1980.

45. Hoffman, "From Surrealism to 'The Apocalypse,' " p. 157.

46. Letter from Moore, 29 September 1980.

47. Ibid.

48. Ibid.
49. Ibid.
50. Ibid.
51. Ibid.
52. Ibid.
53. Note from Hendry, 6 October 1980.
54. Letter from Moore, 19 August, 1980.
55. Letter from Comfort, 11 September 1980.
56. From the Comfort collection of correspondence and publication of the University College, London.
57. Note from Hendry, 6 October 1980.
58. Letter from Moore, 29 September 1980.
59. Ibid.
60. Letter from Moore, 6 November 1980.
61. Ibid.
62. Nicholas Moore, *Recollections of the Gala: Selected Poems, 1943–1948* (London: Editions Poetry, 1950), pp. 24–25.
63. Scarfe, *Auden and After*, p. 166.
64. Nicholas Moore, *The Cabaret, the Dancer, the Gentlemen* (London: Fortune Press, 1942), pp. 42–43.
65. Jean-Paul Sartre, *Being and Nothingness: An Essay on Phenomenological Ontology*, tr. Hazel E. Barnes (New York: Philosophical Library, 1956), p. 87.
66. Moore, *Recollections of the Gala*, p. 56.
67. Ibid., pp. 73–74.
68. Ibid., p. 65.
69. Ibid., p. 29.
70. Letter, 29 September 1980.
71. Nicholas Moore, *Buzzing Around with a Bee and Other Poems* (London, 1941), p. 9.
72. Conversation with Tambimuttu, January 1982.
73. 11 September 1980, letter from Comfort.

Chapter Five

1. Letter from Comfort, 28 August 1980.
2. Baggerly, "Henry Treece," p. 62.
3. Letter from Gardiner, 22 November 1980.
4. From Hendry's files.
5. Baggerly, "Henry Treece," p. 63.
6. Treece and Schimanski, *Transformation Two* (London: L. Drummond, 1944), p. 2.

7. Kenneth Rexroth, *The Phoenix and the Tortoise* (Norfolk: New Directions, 1944), p. 24.

8. Ibid., p. 11.

9. Conversation with Gascoyne, 5 April 1981.

10. Herbert Read, *Education Through Art* (New York: Pantheon Books, 1956), p. 71.

11. Betty Edwards, *Drawing on the Right Side of the Brain* (Los Angeles: J. P. Tarcher, 1979), pp. 35–36.

12. Treece and Schimanski, *Transformation Two,* p. 71 (see also p. 35 of Edwards, *Drawing*).

13. Ibid., p. 2.

14. Ibid., p. 5.

15. Ibid., p. 72.

16. Treece, ed., *Herbert Read,* p. 36.

17. Ibid., p. 111.

18. Herbert Read, *Annals of Innocence and Experience* (New York: Haskell, 1974), pp. 90–91.

19. D. S. Savage, *The Personal Principle: Studies in Modern Poetry* (London: Routledge, 1944), pp. 7–8.

20. Schimanski and Treece, *New Romantic Anthology,* p. 24.

21. Read, *Annals,* p. 90.

22. Carl Rogers, *On Becoming a Person: A Therapist's View of Psychotherapy* (Boston: Houghton Mifflin Co., 1961), p. 188.

23. Stefan Schimanski and Henry Treece, *Transformation (one)* (London: Victor Gollancz, 1943), p. 15.

24. Ibid., p. 140.

25. George Woodcock, *The Writer and Politics* (London: Porcupine Press, 1948), p. 24.

26. Erich Fromm, *Escape From Freedom* (New York: Farrar and Rinehart, 1941), p. 283.

27. Herbert Read, *The Philosophy of Modern Art* (London: Faber and Faber, 1964), p. 75.

28. Herbert Read, *Wordsworth* (London, 1930), p. 179.

29. Rogers, *On Becoming a Person,* pp. 164, 166.

30. Hendry, *Crown and the Sickle,* p. 16.

31. Lawrence, *Apocalypse,* p. 100; Hendry, *White Horseman,* p. v.

32. Schimanski and Treece, *Transformation Three,* pp. 10, 11.

Chapter Six

1. Herbert Read in *Anarchy and Order: Essays in Politics* (Boston: Beacon Press, 1971), p. 58.

2. Letter from Fred Marnau, 16 February 1982. Marnau notes that he is a monarchist, as well as an anarchist, ". . . because I believe that the dignity and liberty of man is never better safeguarded than under a constitutional monarchy" (Ibid.).

3. Kenneth Patchen, in *Poetry Folios,* ed. Alex Comfort and Peter Wells (Barnett: The Editors, 1942), p. 10.

4. Savage, *Personal Principle,* p. 33.

5. William Morris, *News From Nowhere,* ed. James Redmond (London: Routledge and Kegan Paul, 1970), p. 65.

6. Hendry, *Crown and the Sickle,* p. 56.

7. Hendry, "Myth and Social Integration," in *White Horseman,* p. 152.

8. Treece, *How I See Apocalypse,* p. 23.

9. Ibid., p. 22.

10. Schimanski and Treece, *Transformation (one),* p. 16.

11. George Woodcock, *New Life to the Land* (London: Freedom Press, 1942), p. 25.

12. Letter from Woodcock, 7 September 1980.

13. Morris, *News From Nowhere,* p. 13.

14. Herbert Read, *Aristotle's Mother: An Imaginary Conversation* (North Harrow: Philip Ward, 1961), p. 5.

15. Treece, *How I See Apocalypse,* p. 16.

16. Ibid., p. 23.

17. William Godwin, *Imogen* (New York: New York Public Library, 1963), p. 59.

18. G. K. Chesterton, *The Man Who Was Thursday* (New York: Modern Library, 1908), p. 14.

19. Treece, *How I See Apocalypse,* pp. 83–84.

20. J. F. Hendry, *Fernie Brae* (Glasgow, 1949), p. 54.

21. Herbert Read, *Education Through Art,* p. 198.

22. Rogers, *On Becoming a Person,* pp. 399, 398.

23. Hulme, "Romanticism and Classicism," p. 5.

24. Rogers, *On Becoming a Person,* pp. 168, 172, 175.

25. William Godwin, *Enquiry Concerning Political Justice* (Oxford: Oxford University Press, 1971), p. 313.

26. In Thoreau's essay on civil disobedience, included in *The Anarchists,* ed. Irving Horowitz (New York: Dell Publishing Co., 1964) pp. 213, 215.

27. Read, *Poetry and Anarchism,* p. 96.

28. University College, London, collection of Comfort's correspondence.

29. Woodcock, *Stream and the Source,* pp. 38–39.

30. Hendry, *Fernie Brae,* p. 54.

31. Wordsworth's "Ode: Intimations of Immortality," ll. 19–23, 179–84.

32. Savage, *Personal Principle,* p. vi.

33. Wordsworth, *Prelude,* 1. 89.

34. Ibid., ll. 95–97.

35. R. W. Sperry, "Hemisphere Deconnection and Unity in Conscious Awareness," in *Scientific Psychology and Social Concern,* ed. Leonard W. Schmaltz (New York: Harper & Row, 1971), p. 75.

36. Sagan, *Dragons,* p. 183; Edwards, *Drawing,* p. 33.

37. Sagan, *Dragons,* p. 189.

38. Read, *Contrary Experience,* pp. 352–53.

39. Treece, *How I See Apocalypse,* p. 17.

40. Spender, *Destructive Element,* p. 228.

41. Shelley, *The Revolt of Islam,* canto IX.

42. Spender, *The Thirties,* p. 73.

43. Ian Hamilton, *A Poetry Chronicle: Essays and Reviews* (London: Faber and Faber, 1973), pp. 83–84.

44. Kathleen Raine, "Vernon Watkins: Poet of Tradition," *Texas Quarterly* 7 (1964):176, 178.

45. Ibid., pp. 174–74.

46. Ibid., p. 173.

47. Philip Larkin, *Vernon Watkins: 1906–1967,* ed. Leslie Norris (London: Faber, 1970), pp. 16, 29–30.

48. Helmstadter, "Apocalyptic Movement," p. 239.

49. Tindall, *Reader's Guide to Dylan Thomas,* p. 24.

50. Letter from Tom Scott, 3 September 1981.

51. Conversation with Gascoyne, 5 April 1981.

Chapter Seven

1. Read, *New Romantic Anthology,* p. 30.

2. Greene, "A Personal Foreword," *The Contrary Experience,* p. 7.

3. Charles Tomlinson, "Poetry Today," in *The Modern Age,* 7:467–68.

4. White in *Crown and the Sickle,* p. 129.

5. Conquest, *New Lines,* p. xiv.

6. Gardiner, *The Once Loved God,* p. 4.

7. Spender, *The Thirties,* pp. 137–38.

8. Albert Camus, *The Rebel: An Essay on Man in Revolt,* tr. Anthony Bower (New York: Vintage Books, 1956), p. viii.

9. Wrey Gardiner, *The Flowering Moment* (London, 1949), p. 31.

10. Hendry, *White Horseman,* p. 158.

11. R. D. Laing, *The Politics of Experience* (New York: Ballantine Books, 1967), p. 65.

Selected Bibliography

PRIMARY SOURCES

1. G. S. Fraser
Poetry

The Fatal Landscape and Other Poems. London: Poetry London, 1943.
Home Town Elegy. London: Editions Poetry, 1944.
Leaves Without a Tree. Tokyo: Hokuseido Press, 1953.
The Traveller Has Regrets and Other Poems. London: Harvill Press, 1948.
Prose
The Modern Writer and His World. New York: Criterion Books, 1955.
News from South America. London: Harvill Press, 1949.
Post-War Trends in English Literature. Tokyo: Hokuseido, 1950.
Three Philosophical Essays. Tokyo: Eibunsha, n.d.

2. J. F. Hendry
Poetry
The Bombed Happiness. London: Routledge, 1942.
The Orchestral Mountain: A Symphonic Elegy. London: Routledge, 1943.
Short Stories
The Blackbird of Ospo: Stories of Jugoslavia. Glasgow: W. Maclellan, 1945.
Editions
The Crown and the Sickle. Edited by J. F. Hendry and Henry Treece. London: P. S. King & Staples, 1944.
The New Apocalypse. Edited by J. F. Hendry and Henry Treece. London: Fortune Press, 1939.
Scottish Short Stories. Edited by Theodora and J. F. Hendry. Edinburgh: Penguin Books, 1943.
The White Horseman: Prose and Verse of the New Apocalypse. London: Routledge, 1941.
Novels
Fernie Brae: A Scottish Childhood. Glasgow: W. Maclellan, 1949.

3. Norman MacCaig
Poetry
Far Cry. London: Routledge, 1943.
The Inward Eye. London: Routledge, 1946.
A Man in My Position. London, 1969.

Riding Lights. New York: Hogarth Press, 1956.

The Sinai Sort. New York: Hogarth Press, 1957.

4. Nicholas Moore

Poetry

A Book for Priscilla: Poems. Cambridge, 1941.

Buzzing Around with a Bee and Other Poems. London: Poetry (London), 1941.

The Cabaret, the Dancer, the Gentlemen: Poems. London: Fortune Press, 1942.

The Glass Tower. London: Poetry (London), 1944.

The Island and the Cattle: Poems. London: Fortune Press, 1941.

Recollections of the Gala: Selected Poems, 1943–1948. London: Editions Poetry London, 1949.

5. Herbert Read

Art and Social Criticism

Art Now: An Introduction to the Theory of Modern Painting and Sculpture. London: Faber & Faber, 1933.

The Cult of Sincerity. New York: Horizon Press, 1969.

Reason and Romanticism. London: Faber and Gwyer, 1926.

To Hell with Culture, and Other Essays in Art and Society. New York: Schocken Books, 1963.

Wordsworth. London: Faber and Faber, 1930.

Editions

Surrealism. London: Faber and Faber, 1936.

Novels

The Green Child. New York: New Directions, 1948.

Poetry

Collected Poems. New York: Faber, 1966.

Autobiographies

The Contrary Experience: Autobiographies. London: Faber and Faber, 1963.

6. Henry Treece

Poetry

The Black Seasons. London: Faber & Faber, 1945.

The Exiles. London: Faber and Faber, 1952.

The Haunted Garden. London: Faber and Faber, 1947.

Invitation and Warning. London: Faber and Faber, 1942.

38 Poems. London: Fortune Press, 1940.

Prose

Dylan Thomas: "Dog Among the Fairies." London: L. Drummond, 1949.

How I See Apocalypse. London: L. Drummond, 1946.

Editions
   Air Force Poetry. Edited by John Pudney and Henry Treece. London: John
      Lane, 1944.
   The Crown and the Sickle. Edited by J. F. Hendry and Henry Treece. Lon-
      don: P. S. King & Staples, 1944.
   Herbert Read: An Introduction to His Work by Various Hands. London: Faber
      and Faber, 1944.
   The New Apocalypse. Edited by J. F. Hendry and Henry Treece. London:
      Fortune Press, 1939.
   Transformation (one)–Four. Edited by Stefan Schimanski and Henry Treece.
      London: L. Drummond, 1943–1946.
   Wartime Harvest: An Anthology of Prose and Verse. Edited by Stefan Schi-
      manski and Henry Treece. London, 1943.
   The White Horseman. Edited by J. F. Hendry and Henry Treece. London:
      Routledge, 1941.

7. Wrey Gardiner
Autobiographies
   The Colonies of Heaven. London: Grey Walls Press, 1941.
   The Dark Thorn. London: Grey Walls Press, 1946.
   The Flowering Moment. London: Grey Walls Press, 1949.
   The Once Loved God. London: Fortune Press, 1943.
Poetry
   The Gates of Silence. London: Grey Walls Press, 1944.
   Lament for Strings. London: Grey Walls Press, 1947.
   Questions for Waking. London: Fortune Press, 1942.

SECONDARY SOURCES

1.   Books and Articles
Hill, E. F. F. "Apocalypse." In *A New Romantic Anthology*. Edited by Stefan
   Schimanski and Henry Treece. London, 1949, pp. 38–50. Demon-
   strates little historical awareness of the historical context and implications of either first-, nineteenth-, or mid-twentieth-century apocalyptic
   mentality. Probably included by Treece and Schimanski because of its
   title and Hill's enthusiasm for the abstract concept of apocalypse from
   a theologized perspective. The reader interested in the concept of apocalypse would be better served by reading Hendry's intelligent essay
   "The Apocalyptic Element in Modern Poetry," *Poetry Scotland* (1945),
   pp. 61–66.
Hoffman, Frederick J. "From Surrealism to 'The Apocalypse': A Devel-

opment in Twentieth Century Irrationalism." *Journal of English Literary History* 15 (1948):147–65. Hoffman's historical survey is interesting and historically important as an early attempt to explain the Apocalyptic Movement, but oversimplified in its conclusion that Treece, Moore, Hendry, and Fraser "called themselves the 'Poets of the Apocalypse,' " rejected the precedent of "Auden and Spender," and "agreed upon" the Apocalyptic "statement of principle" or manifesto. Also oversimplified is Hoffman's view that in "the poetry of the Apocalypse, one discovers a mood of personal resignation to the brutality of modern life, combined with skepticism regarding any confident prophets of world order."

Lindsay, Jack. Sections entitled "Herbert Read" (pp. 15–17), "Apocalyptics" (pp. 17–18), and "Myth" (pp. 24–26), in particular, in his *Perspective for Poetry*. London, 1944. Contains both misleading oversimplifications and illogical conclusions about the poets treated. Presented in pretentious, propagandistic diction, but of some historical interest as showing wartime partly Freudian attitudes toward Read and Apocalypticism from the point of view of an enthusiastic Marxist true believer.

Morgan, Walford. "Notes on Contemporary Tendencies: the Apocalyptic School." In *A New Romantic Anthology*. Edited by Stefan Schimanski and Henry Treece. London: Grey Walls Press, 1949, pp. 51–58. More informed and less pretentious than Hill or Lindsay, Morgan presents sound conclusions about Apocalypticism's debt to Read and the Surrealists together with doctrinaire, unsupported pronouncements on Read's reverent agnosticism.

Scarfe, Francis. *Auden and After: The Liberation of Poetry, 1930–41*. London: George Routledge & Sons, 1942. Scarfe's book is of interest as an early attempt to write about poetry of the post-Eliot period, and it contains a generally helpful chapter on the Apocalyptic Movement.

Spender, Stephen. "Lessons of Poetry 1943." *Horizon* 9, no. 51 (1944):207–16. A perceptive, intelligently written essay, covering Hendry, Gascoyne, Savage, MacCaig, Woodcock, etc., based on Spender's preference for the "crystalline clarity" and "gemlike" quality of Raine and others in contrast to the often less economical use of language (cf. Comfort's sensible comment on the fault of "excessive adjectives" in contemporary Romanticism, *A New Romantic Anthology*, p. 93) and the disturbing "extraordinary vagueness" of some of the New Romantics.

Stanford, Derek. *The Freedom of Poetry*. London, 1947. Of special interest as literary criticism written by a Neo-Romantic and contemporary of the writers discussed. Contains entire chapters on Moore, Gardiner, Comfort, Keyes, and other poets of the 1940s.

2. Dissertations

Baggerly, Jo Ann. "Henry Treece and the New Apocalypse: A Study of English Neo-Romanticism." Ph.D. diss., Texas Technological University, 1973. Recommended only for the most ardent students of Neo-Romanticism. Baggerly does not acknowledge Helmstadter's dissertation (below) and does not adequately acknowledge her sources. Contains factual errors.

Helmstadter, Thomas Hicks. "The Apocalyptic Movement in British Poetry." Ph.D. diss., University of Pennsylvania, 1963. Provides generally competent, sensible, and accurate treatment of the Apocalyptic Movement. Copies of letters to Henry Treece used in my analysis were most graciously provided by Mrs. Francis Helmstadter from her late husband's personal files.

Index

adjustment psychology, 127–28
"Advertisement" for the Second Manifese Du Surréalisme" (Breton), 25
"After the Funeral" (Thomas), 36
Air Force Poetry, 57
Aldington, Richard, 12–13
alienation, 111
alienated labor, 93
Altarwise by Owl-Light (Thomas), 47
Amis, Kingsley, 117, 119, 120
anarchism, 90, 91, 92, 95, 97, 98, 117, 127, 128; and monarchism, 92; and power, 98; and social change through personal redemption, 107; tree as a metaphor for, 96–97
anarchist, communism, 95; as defined by Sir Herbert Read, 98; experience universalized, 111; mentality, 84; popular image of, 91, 127; theorists, 105; view of history, 110–11
anarchists, 95, 109, 125; pacifist, 6, 43, 111
Anarchy or Chaos (Woodcock), 91
Annals of Innocence and Experience (Read), 88, 100
apocalypse, and Jewish eschatology, 24, 25, 37; miniaturized, 45; as personal revelation, 38, 59; cf. depth psychology
Apocalypse (Lawrence), 24, 25, 42, 90
"Apocalypse and Resurrection"

(Bayliss), 109, 113; influenced by the New Apocalypse, 109
"Apocalypse in Poetry" (Fraser), 18, 19
Apocalypse Now, 5
Apocalyptic anthologies, 43, 77, 117; magazine, 77; manifesto, 3, 4, 23, 26, 66
Apocalyptic art, humor, wit, and irony in, 75–76—Cf. 119, 120; imagery of, 14, 18, 24; and Neo-Romantic rebellion, 8–9; style, 9; violence in, 105
apocalyptic dream visions, 48, 58, 70
"Apocalyptic Element in Modern Poetry, The" (Hendry), 62
apocalyptic imagery, 39, 113, 114, 115; and the end of the world, 24–25, 115; metamorphosed sexually, 63; as a projection of an internal metamorphosis or rebirth, 37; and time and space dilating or collapsing, 114
apocalyptic literature, 73; beasts and dragons in, 20–21, 52; conventional elements of, 20; masses of people in, 72–73; mountain symbols in, 36; optimism and pessimism in, 109; writers of, 20, 103–104
apocalyptic visions, 20, 25, 72, 103–104, 111; of disaster, 24–25, 89; ghostly visitant in, 59–60; poet-prophet as mentally

deranged in, 48; poet-seer in,
58, 59, 108–109, 115; as projections of death anxiety, 45–
46—cf. 24, 114; symbolic of anomie, 24; and world war, 24–25,
46

Apocalypticism, 1–3, 5, 9, 10, 11,
18, 19, 23, 24, 25, 26, 46, 53,
62, 65, 66, 67, 69, 84, 85, 89,
103, 105, 111, 115, 123; reaction against—*See* Neo-Romanticism and *New-Lines* Movement;
and Surrealism, 18–19, 23;
Treece's development away from,
55–56

Apocalyptics, 112; the New Apocalyptics and their "unchecked
rhetoric," 116

Aristotle's Mother (Read), 94

Art and Letters, 11

Art and Social Responsibility (Comfort), 91, 105

Art Now, 10

Auden, W. H., 9, 39, 70, 77, 78,
80, 93, 99, 106

Auden group poets, 9, 10, 18, 19,
44, 77, 91, 93, 95, 103

"Author's Prologue" (Thomas), 36

ballad form, revival of, 53–54

Baker, Peter, 6, 129n23

Bakunin, Mikhail, 98

Barbarism and Sexual Freedom (Comfort), 126

Barker, George, 6, 7, 9, 14, 18,
19, 25, 36, 39, 44, 47, 48, 49,
52, 53, 58–59, 63, 64, 67, 71,
72, 73, 76, 77, 80, 99, 102,
103, 111, 114, 122

bartering, 93

Battle of Britian, 8

Bayliss, John, 6, 18, 19, 55–56,
57, 76, 77, 92, 109

Beckett, Samuel, 25

Behaviorism, 123

Being and Nothingness (Sartre), 81

Blake, William, 16, 35, 48, 52,
59, 63, 80, 89, 96, 99, 110,
111, 112, 117

Blok, Alexander, 85

"Bombing Casualties in Spain"
(Read), 77, 85

Breton, André, 18, 19, 25, 111,
115; and Mme. Breton, 18, 19

"Broken Sea, The" (Watkins), 108,
112–14

Buber, Martin, 86

"Buntingsdale" (Woodcock),
101–102

Bunyan, John, 36

"Burning Babe, The" (Thomas), 4, 51

Byron, George Gordon, 55, 70

Byronic narrator, 48

Caleb Williams (Godwin), 106

Camus, Albert, 10, 67, 69, 70,
106, 123–24, 127

Capitalism, 78, 93, 126—*See* sharing, 94

Carlyle, Thomas, 98, 117

Caton, 4–5, 76, 77

centralization, 36

Churchill, Winston, 17

Classical and Neo-Classical, ideals,
117; normative assumptions, 90;
social roles, 119; traits, 105

Classicism and Romanticism and
Neo-Romanticism, oscillations,
122

Cocteau, Jean, 55–56

Coleridge, S. T., 13, 35, 36, 44,
47–48, 55, 56, 59, 63, 65, 111

Coleridgean narrator—*See* Byronic narrator

Collins, Cecil, 77, 85

Comfort, Alex, 4–5, 6, 7, 8–9, 10–11, 19, 43, 44, 47, 53, 54, 70, 76, 77, 80, 84, 92, 93, 97, 99, 105–106, 107, 111, 122, 127

Communism, 77, 93

Conquest, Robert, 116–17

Conrad, Joseph, 127

Contrary Experience, The (Read), 104

Cooke, Dorian, 1–2, 3, 4, 8, 25, 30, 51–52

Crown and the Sickle, The, 5, 55, 56, 85, 90, 103, 105, 116; symbolic implications of the title, 103

Dali, Salvador, 17, 18, 46

"Dark Horse of the Apocalypse, The" (Orwell), 19

Davies, Hugh Sykes, 19

death, utopian compensation for, 108

"Death of Kropotkin, The" (Read), 105

decentralization, 94, 128; and communal collectives, 93

demented persona, 43

depersonalization, 93, 98, 128

depth psychology, 18–19, 123–24—*See* 60–61; Jungian, 15–16; Freudian, 97, 122

Dickens, Charles, 100

Dimond, Stuart, 104

Dominguez, Oscar, 46

Dostoevsky, Feodor, 26

Dragons of Eden, The (Sagan), 19–20

dream visions, 21; Cf. 30, 35, 36; format revived, 58

Dreiser, Theodore, 78

Dryden, John, 9

Duino Elegies (Rilke), 30–31

Eden, private and communal, 110—*See* Golden Age

"Education and Art" (Read), 86–88

Education and Art (Read), 86, 96–97

education, theories of, 85–88, 96–97; and hemispheral specialization, 87

Edwards, Betty, 87, 104

"Elegy V" (Barker), 47

"Elegy for a Girl Dead in an Air-Raid" (Comfort), 114

"Elegy No. I" (Barker), 52, 58, 63–64, 72, 114

Eliot, T. S., 9, 11–12, 13, 19, 25, 43, 44, 47, 48, 50, 58, 59, 67, 72, 97, 112, 113, 117, 125; at Faber & Gwyer, 12; his conversion, 12

Ellis, Albert, 123, 126

Eluard, Paul, 62, 111, 125, 126

"Epistle I" (Barker), 53

"Especially When the October Wind" (Thomas), 46

"Eve of St. Agony or the Middle-class Was Sitting on Its Fat" (Patchen), 92

Existence and Being (Heidegger), 81

Existentialism, 26, 27, 46, 52, 67, 68, 69, 120, 123, 127; and authenticity, 72; *See* Neo-Romanticism and Existentialism

Ewart, Gavin, 75

Eysenck, H. J., 124

"Ezra Pound's Guilt" (Patchen), 92

"Factory" (Savage), 98

Falcon Press, 6

"False Return, The" (Heath-
Stubbs), 112, 113
Fear of Freedom, The (Fromm), 90
"Fern Hill" (Thomas), 100, 101
"First Elegy" (Comfort), 100
Flint, F. S., 12
Flowering Moment, The (Gardiner),
127
Fortune Anthology, The, 76–77
Fortune Press, 5, 76
Forster, E. M., 125
four horsemen of the apocalypse,
108
Fraser, G. S., 1, 4, 9, 10, 11,
13–14, 17, 18, 19, 26, 36–37,
66–73, 103

WORKS—FICTION:
"Inside Story," 67

WORKS—POETRY:
"Crisis," 70–72
Leaves Without a Tree, 70
"Letter to Nicholas Moore, A,"
70

WORKS—PROSE:
Three Philosophical Essays, 66–69

Fraser, Paddy, 66
Freedom Press, 125
Freud, Lucian, and Nicholas
Moore, 74
Freud, Sigmund, 23, 26, 27, 32,
63, 64, 71, 79, 91, 101, 102,
123; Freudian ambiguity, 44
Fromm, Erich, 89, 90, 105, 123
Fuller, Roy, 7

Gant, Roland, 6
Gardiner, Wrey, 5, 6, 7–8, 9, 10,
16, 17, 19, 73, 74, 76, 77, 85,
92, 93, 95, 97, 118

Gascoyne, David, 17, 19, 25, 52,
62, 97, 105, 115; and Martin
Buber, 86; movement away from
Surrealism, 86
"Gates of Silence, The" (Gardiner),
121
Genet, Jean, 18
Giono, Jean, 125, 126
Godwin, Mary Wollstonecraft, 127
Godwin, William, 27, 89, 90, 94,
95, 98, 105, 106, 107, 109, 119
Goldman, Emma, 126–27
Golden Age or Eden, 20, 94, 95,
100, 110; renewed, 110, 111;
and biological evolution of the
brain, 20; Cf. Messianic King-
dom, 24; Kingdom of God, 106,
internalized, 107–108, demy-
thologized, 107, and romantic
love, 107–108
Goodland, John, 1, 2, 3, 4, 23,
25, 76
Goodman, Paul, 7, 92, 96,
105–106, 127, 128
gothicism, in Thomas and Treece,
51, 54
Greacen, Robert, 6, 9
Green Child, The (Read), 15–16,
94, 97, 99, 100, 101, 106, 118
Grey Walls Press, 6, 7, 76, 85
Greene, Graham, 116
Grigson, Jeoffrey, 129n25
Grosz, Georg, 61
Gunn, Thomas, 70

"Hangman's Great Hands, The"
(Patchen), 92
Hardy, Thomas, 66, 69, 79
Heath-Stubbs, John, 112, 113
Heidegger, Martin, 25, 46, 70,
81, 82

Hemingway, Ernest, 65
Hendry, James F., 1, 2, 3, 4, 5,
6, 8, 10, 14, 16, 17, 18, 19,
23–42, 43, 44, 52, 53, 56, 59,
62, 66, 67, 73, 75–76, 77, 85,
88, 89, 90, 92, 93, 95, 96, 97,
100, 108, 111, 112, 113, 116–
17, 121, 125, 127

WORKS—FICTION:
"Caves of Altamira, The," 31–32
"Chrysalis," 27–28
Fernie Brae: a Scottish Childhood,
96, 100

WORKS—POETRY:
"Adonai," 41–42
"Apocalypse," 39
Bombed Happiness, The, 30
"Death of Milton, The," 40
"Golgotha," 34, 39
"John Ball, Priest, to the Nation
(1382)," 92, 93, 127
"London Before Invasion," 39,
112
"Midnight Air-Raid," 38–39
"Ode on a Chinese Scroll," 41
Orchestral Mountain, The, 28–38,
53, 59, 72
"Portrait of David," 29
"Prelude to a Ballad for Heroes,"
113
"Reflex of History, The," 40

Hendry, Theodora, 8—*See* J. F.
Hendry's *The Orchestral Mountain*
Herbert Read: An Introduction to His
Works by Various Hands (ed.,
Treece), 13, 43, 88
Herring, Robert, 85
Hirohito, 17
Hitler, Adolf, 17, 26, 89, 91

"Holy Poems" (Barker), 36, 39,
58–59
Horney, Karen, 89
Hulme, T. S., 11, 12, 13, 19, 97
Huxley, Aldous, 17, 40

"I DON'T WANT TO STARTLE
YOU but they are going to kill
most of us" (Patchen), 125
I and Thou (Buber), 86
"I See the Boys of Summer"
(Thomas), 101
"If I Were Tickled By the Rub of
Love" (Thomas), 47, 50
Imagism, 12–14, 44
Imogen (Godwin), 94, 106, 107; on
decentralized communities, 94

Jaspers, Carl, 17
Johnson, Samuel, 9, 93
Journal of Albion Moonlight
(Patchen), 125
Journey to the Border (Upward), 61
Joy of Sex, The (Comfort), 126
Jung, Carl, 15–16, 19, 21, 35,
38, 71, 89, 90, 101, 112

Kafka, Franz, 25, 27, 28, 29, 45,
51, 61, 65
Keats, John, 41, 55, 56, 83
Keyes, Sidney, 9, 74, 77
Kierkegaard, Sören, 27, 69, 90
Kingdom Come, 7, 85
Kropotkin, Peter, 15, 43, 91–92,
98, 105, 127

Laing, R. D., 127
"Lament for Strings" (Gardiner), 16
"Landscape of the Mind"
(Gardiner), 121
Langland, William, 73

Larkin, Philip, 112, 120, 121,
    122, 124, 125
law, 94
Lawrence, D. H., 18, 24, 25, 32,
    37, 42, 57, 90, 118
"Legend" (Bayliss), 55
Levertov, Denise, 6, 8, 73
Lewis, C. Day, 9, 38, 93, 99
Lewis, Wyndham, 12
"Light Breaks Where No Sun
    Shines" (Thomas), 49
"Lost Princess, The" (Bayliss), 55
Lyra: An Anthology of New Lyric, 6

MacCaig, Norman, 1, 3, 17, 19,
    62–66, 67, 118

    WORKS—POETRY:
    "Birds All Singing," 66, 118
    Far Cry, 64–65, 17
    "Nine Poems," 62–64, 66
    "No Escape," 66
    Riding Lights, 66

machine age, 3, 4
MacNeice, Louis, 9, 16, 83, 84,
    93, 99
Magritte, René, 46
Maltese Falcon, The, 124
"Mame de Carseau, La" (Eluard),
    62
Man Who Was Thursday, The (Ches-
    terton), 91, 96, 127
"Mana" (Watkins), 111
Mannin, Ethel, 125
Mansfield, Katherine, 8
"Map of Love, The" (Thomas), 76
Marcel, Gabriel, 67, 68
Marcuse, Herbert, 126
Marnau, Alfred, 92, 138n2
"Martyrdom of the House, The"
    (Comfort), 105

Marx, Karl, 93, 94, 95
Marxism and anarchism, 93
Marxist mentality, 84, 91
Maslow, Abraham, 38, 68, 89, 97,
    99, 123
Masson, André, 19
May, Rollo, 123
mechanic and organic, 38, 98
mechanization, 128; and punish-
    ment, 98; and spontaneity in be-
    havior and art, 98, 99
medievalism, 55
Melville, Robert, 85
Mein Kampf (Hitler), 26, 89
Mill, John Stuart, 69
Miller, Henry, 49, 85
"Mr. Symons at Richmond, Mr.
    Pope at Twickenham" (Symons),
    109
Moore, G. E., 73–75
Moore, Nicholas, 1, 2, 3, 4, 6–8,
    9, 10, 23, 25, 36, 43, 62, 64,
    66, 70, 73–84, 103, 108; his at-
    titude towards the New Apoca-
    lypse, 2, 75–76, 77

    WORKS—POETRY:
    "Epistle to H. T. (for Henry
        Treece)," 78–79
    Glass Tower, The, 74
    "Hair's Breadth, The," 80–81
    "Indian and the Shark, The,"
        83–84
    "Lovers Under the Elms," 81
    "Mountain and the Valley, The
        (for Priscilla)," 80
    "Nostalgia," 79
    "Ode to Fear," 82–83
    "Prayer to Nobody, Who is
        Something (for Priscilla)," 80
    "Recollection," 83
    "River in the Sun, The," 108

"Ruin and the Sun, The," 77–78
"Salutation for Theodore Dreiser, A," 78
"Suitable Emotions," 81–82
"Who See the Coming of the Morning," 78

Moore, Thomas Sturge Moore, 75
Morris, William, 92, 94
Mounier, Emmanuel, 85, 86
"Mummy, The" (Watkins), 111
Munch, Edvard, 61
Murray, John Middleton, 8, 125
Mussolini, Benito, 17
Mutual Aid (Kropotkin), 92
myth, 4, 27, 78, 90; mythical mode of development, 11
Myth of Sisyphus, The (Camus), 106

nature, 10, 99; imagery, 25; impressionistic responses to, 121; indifference or hostility of, 10; Neo-Romantic fascination with, 117; numinosity of, 9
Neo-Classicism, late 17th- and 18th-century, 9, 103, 121
Neo-Classicism, modern, 98, 119; Eliot dominated, 9, 11, 19
Neo-Classical poetry, 18th-century, 118; 18th-century and modern, 104–105; *See* Neo-Augustan, 66, 70
Neo-Romantic, archetypes, 15–16, 19–22, 35, 121; art, 52; concerns, 127, 128; forerunners, 6; language distortions and psychosis, 61; manifesto, 105; medievalism, 122, 124; obscurity, 117; obsessions, 19–20; poetry, 10, 13, 25, 44; poets, 5–6, 9, 10, 11, 16, 17, 18, 19, 44, 111; process mentality, 38, 97;

style, 97; symbolism, 117; works, 48; writers, 26–27, 28, 63, 93, 97, 115, 118, 119
Neo-Romantic imagery, 13, 19, 117, 118; artificial and natural, 9–10, 25; cinematographic qualities of, 14; nightmarish quality of, 18, 52; and psychosis, 61
Neo-Romantic rebellion or revolt, 8–9, 11–12, 72, 104, 120; versus revolution, 106
Neo-Romantic and *New-Lines* Movement poetry; and direct expression of emotion, 120; detachment, 120; realism, 120; time, 121
Neo-Romanticism and Existentialism, 46, 106, 127; *See* individual writers—Sartre, Camus, etc.
Neo-Romanticism, 1–10, 26, 46, 97; allusions in, 44; ambiguity in, 44; autonomy as a goal, 97; complexity (syntactical and symbolic) of, 44; consciousness expanding in, 17; death in, 20; and deconditioning, 99; emotionally charged states experienced simultaneously in, 101; environment in, 46; and the expected German invasion, 39–40; high-dominance fantasies in, 100; Imagism's influence on, 13, 14; integration of the psyche in, 47–48, 83, 84, 87, 88, 102–105; 116–17, 122, 128— Cf. perceptual integration, 42; Kafka's influence on, 28; nature symbolism in, 50, 110—*See* nature; primitive character of, 16; primitivism in, 16, 102; primitive diction of, 49; Prometheanism in, 11; reaction against,

116–26; reconciling Romanticism and Classicism in, 12, 104–105; self-limiting tendencies of, 118; and science, 105; and objectivity, 105, 122, 123; tone (social and personal) of, 15; rhetoric in, 116, 117; violence and terror in, 52, 105; visionary utopianism of, 117, 122

Neo-Romanticism and Romanticism, 17, 18, 19, 27, 40, 47, 48, 88–89, 96, 97, 98; childhood in, 21–22, 99–102—and Freudianism, 122; and creative passivity and spontaniety, 19, 31—See 87; and evolution, 12; gloom and hemispheral specialization in, 104; imagination in, 47–48—Cf. imagination and reason, 103–104, 118; and Imagism, 12–13, 117; and Neo-Classicism, 93; functional lateralization as a possible basis for, 104–105; and optimism, 27; and polymorphism, 90; physiological basis for Romantic and Classical alternations, 104–105; reactions against Classicism, 93; and self-actualization, 38, 89; self-destructive tendencies in, 119; and sexual polarization and male domination, 119–20; and sexual and aggressive instincts linked, 63; and social roles, 119–20, 124; and victimization, 106; view of the artist, 16–17

Neo-Romanticism, Romanticism, and anarchism, 91–111—See 120; and self-expression, 119; and integration with the community, 110; and process mentality applied to politics, 106; and rationalism, 119; and renewal imagery, 110–11; and science, 119

New Apocalypse, The, 2, 4, 5, 19, 23, 45, 51, 61, 76, 100, 116–17

"New Heaven and a New Earth, A" (Lawrence), 37

New Life to the Land (Woodcock), 94

New Lines: An Anthology, 116

New-Lines Movement poetry, 97, 116–23; characteristics of, 120; imagery of, 118

New Poetry, The, 65

New Road: New Directions in European Art and Letters, 6, 7, 57, 92, 125, 126

New Romantic Anthology, A, 3, 18, 88, 61, 80, 105, 116

New Verse, 129n25

News from Nowhere (Morris), 88, 92, 94

Newton, Denny, 76, 77

Nietzsche, Friedrich, 26, 27, 88, 89

"Night" (Read), 13

Nin, Anaïs, 85

"None But My Foe to Be My Guide" (Comfort), 111, 125–26

Now, 7, 8, 88

"Now (for Elizabeth)" (Woodcock), 94

"Ode Without Rhetoric" (Read), 15

Odets, Clifford, 24

Oelze, Richard, 46

On Becoming a Person (Rogers), 89

Onced Loved God, The (Gardiner), 16, 122

Orage, Richard, 11

"Orchard and the Sin, The" (Stanford), 48
Orwell, George, 17, 19

pacifism, 78
Paradox of Anarchism, The (Read), 91
Pascal, Blaise, 119
Pasternak, Boris, 85
Patchen, Kenneth, 17, 18, 52, 85, 92, 99, 111, 122, 125
Pater, Walter, 70
Pavlov, Ivan, 40, 123
Pearl poet, 30, 35, 73
Penguin Book of Scottish Short Stories, The, 31
Perls, Fritz, 123, 128
Personal Principle: Studies in Modern Poetry (Savage), 88, 92, 103
Personalism, 67, 85–90, 105; and Apocalypticism, 85, 90
personality, escape from, 119; and character, 67, 68–69; *See* Personalism
Petron (Davies), 19
Phases of English Poetry (Read), 10
Phoenix, 126
Phoenix and the Tortoise, The (Rexroth), 86
Pinter, Harold, 25
"Poem for September, 1939" (Woodcock), 39
"Poem for the Sane" (Gardiner), 119
"Poem from London, 1941" (Woodcock), 111
"Poem in Memory of Theodora Hendry" (Cooke), 30
"Poem in October" (Thomas), 50, 101
Poetry and Truth (Eluard), 126
Poetry Folios, 6, 7, 92

poetry, incantatory, 111
Poetry (London), 6–7, 129–30n25
Poetry Quarterly, 5, 6, 7, 53
political revolution, non-violent, 107
Politics and the Unpolitical (Read), 10
Politics of Experience, The (Laing), 127
Pope, Alexander, 9, 70, 93
Portrait of the Artist as a Young Dog, The (Thomas), 76
Pound, Ezra, 12, 13, 44, 54, 93
precognition, 28, 29, 30
primary-group controls, 94
Princess Casamassima, The (James), 127
Proudhon, Pierre J., 105

Raine, Kathleen, 7, 111–12
Ramuz, Charles-Ferdinand, 25
"Ray Scarpe: Part I: The Man from the Vision of Nothing" (Cooke), 51–52
Read, Herbert, 5, 7, *10–16,* 18–19, 27, 40, 43, 46, 66, 67, 88, 89, 93, 94, 95, 96, 97, 98, 99, 101, 102, 104, 105, 106, 111, 112, 115, 116, 117, 118, 119, 122, 125, 126, 127, 128; and Gestalt psychology, 86–87
Reason and Romanticism (Read), 10, 12
Rebel, The (Camus), 127
"Refusal to Mourn the Death, by Fire, of a Child in London, A" (Thomas), 113–14
Refusal to Obey (Giono), 126
Reich, Wilhelm, 88, 126
Religion and the Modern Mind (Stace), 86
"Resolution of Dependence"

(Barker), 71–72, 103
Rexroth, Kenneth, 1, 7, 86, 127
Rhys, Keidrych, 3
Ridler, Anne, 85
Rilke, Rainer Maria, 25, 30–31,
    52
Robeson, Paul, 78
Rogers, Carl, 68, 89, 90, 97, 123,
    128
Romantic; journey motif revived,
    48—See 60–61; theory of the
    self, 68; vision-is-fled theme re-
    vived, 56
Roosevelt, F. D., 17
Routledge & Kegan Paul, 5, 10
Ruskin, John, 65

Sagan, Carl, 19, 20, 104, 110
Sartre, Jean-Paul, 26, 27, 64, 67,
    68, 69, 79, 81, 114, 124
Savage, D. S., 7, 8, 9, 85, 88, 92,
    94, 98, 103, 126; as a Christian
    Personalist, 88; on Read and Ro-
    manticism, 88
Scarfe, Francis, 85
Schimanski, Stefan, 1, 2, 15, 43,
    67, 80, 85, 86, 87, 88, 89, 90,
    93–94, 105
Schweitzer, Albert, 24
Scott, Tom, 66, 103, 115
Shelley, Percy Bysshe, 13, 17, 27,
    39, 52, 55, 59, 66, 73, 89, 95,
    98, 106, 107, 108, 109, 111,
    112, 118, 128; and cosmic pos-
    turing, 13
"Should Lanterns Shine" (Thomas),
    111, 119
Sitwell, Osbert, 76; Osbert and
    Sacheverell Sitwell, 12
"Sixth Elegy" (Comfort), 72
Secret Agent, The (Conrad), 127
"Secular Elegy V" (Barker), 49

Seven, 1, 76
"Seven Dreams" (Bayliss), 19
Sex in Society (Comfort), 126
sexual; poetry, 80, 83, 102; polari-
    zation, 119, 120; bias, 120
sexuality, non-repressive; and an-
    archism, Romanticism, and Neo-
    Romanticism, 105; and the New
    Morality, 126–27
Skinner, B. F., 90, 123
sociopathology, 127
"Song for the Spanish Anarchists,
    A" (Read), 95–96
Spender, Stephen, 9, 12, 14,
    24–25, 39, 40, 41, 44, 70, 77,
    85, 93, 94, 95, 106, 110, 112,
    126
Sperry, R. W., 87, 104, 105
Stace, W. T., 86
Stalin, Joseph, 91, 92
Stanford, Derek, 19, 48, 53, 77,
    93
Stevens, Wallace, 76
"Sunday on Hampstead Heath"
    (Woodcock), 109–11
Supervielle, Jules, 18
Surrealism, 13, 18, 19, 26, 34,
    48, 52, 54, 61, 62, 65, 66, 68,
    91, 97, 98, 117; and Apocalyp-
    ticism as a development from,
    19; and creative passivity and
    spontaneity, 19; cosmic imagery
    of as an influence, 64; and end-
    of-the-world imagery, 25; and
    Neo-Romantic death conscious-
    ness, 46
Surrealism, 18
"Surrealism and the Romantic Prin-
    ciple" (Read), 18
Surrealists, 19, 63, 118, 127;
    imaginative environment, 65
Symons, Julian, 7, 8, 109, 129n25

Tambimuttu, J. Meary, 6–7, 8, 84, 129n25
Thomas, Dylan, 2, 3, 4, 5, 6, 7, 9, 10, 14, 18, 19, 23, 25, 34, 36, 37, 43, 44, 46, 47, 49, 52, 54, 61, 62, 64, 74, 76, 77, 80, 91, 99, 105, *111–14*, 119; attitude towards the New Apocalypse, 4, 111
Thoreau, Henry D., 98
Threshold, The, 76
"Tike" (Breton), 34
"To a Conscript of 1940" (Read), 14
Tolstoy, Leo, 43, 98
"Tout Paradis n'est pas Perdu" (Breton), 47
Transformation (one), 67, 89, 93–94
Transformation Two, 86, 87, 88
Treece, Henry, 1, 2, 3, 4, 5, 6, 7, 8–9, 10–11, 13, 14, 15, 16, 17, 18, 19, 21, 22, 25, 26, 34, 36, 38, 40, *43–61,* 62, 66, 67, 68, 71, 72, 73, 74, 75–76, 77, 78, 80, 88, 89, 90, 93–94, 95, 96, 97, 98, 99, 100, 101, 102, 103, 104, 105, 106–107, 108, 111, 113, 118, 121, 124, 127

WORKS—FICTION:
"Brindled Cow, The," 43

WORKS—POETRY:
Ballad of the Prince, The, 21, 53–55
Black Seasons, The, 55
"Mystic Numbers," 34
"Never-Ending Rosary, The," 98
"Oh Child," 100
"Pastoral," 9, 66
"Poem" (beginning "After a little while"), 50, 100
"Poem" (beginning "When Spring's caress"), 21
"Remembering Last Year," 53, 101
"Resurrection (Part I)," 54
Selections from a Poem in Progress, 48, 96
"Speech for Hamlet," 50–51
Thirty-Eight Poems, review of, 19
"To the Edge and Back," 55–60, 71, 72, 108, 121
Towards a Personal Armageddon, 38, 46–48, 60, 98
"Y Ddraig Goch," 21–22, 102

WORKS—PROSE:
Dylan Thomas: "Dog Among the Fairies," 43
How I See Apocalypse, 43, 57, 62, 93, 94, 96, 106–107

True Confessions of George Barker, The (Barker), 102, 122
Twentieth-Century Verse, 129n25

Unamuno, de, Miguel, 25
Upward, Edward, 61
urbanization, 36,
usury, 93

Van Gogh, Vincent, 61
"Vision of England '38" (Barker), 48, 59, 72
Vogel, Philip, 104

"Waiting for the Wind" (Comfort), 39
Walpole, Horace, 51
"Waterloo Bridge" (Woodcock), 59, 60, 107–109, 112
Watkins, Vernon, 5, 6, 9, 108, 111–14
Watson, John, 17, 27, 123
Welch, Denton, 44

Wells, Peter, 6, 7

West, Nathanael, 65

Wolfe, Thomas, 102

women; attitudes towards, 119–20; emancipation of, 126–27; male confusion about, 80

Woodcock, George, 6, 7, 8, 10, 12, 43, 89, 92, 94, 95, 98, 101, 102, 107–11, 112, 122, 127

Wordsworth (Read), 90, 116

Wordsworth, William, 9, 13, 16, 25, 40, 44, 48, 52, 53, 56, 59, 71, 72, 74, 86, 89, 97, 98, 99, 101, 102, 103, 108, 113

White Horseman, The, 13, 18, 27, 36–37, 62, 64, 66, 76, 77, 90, 93, 99, 103, 111

White, Terrence, 116

Williams, Oscar, 5, 57

writer's block, 115

Yeats, W. B., 9, 21, 24, 26

DATE DUE

GAYLORD			PRINTED IN U.S.A.